WOLVERINE

WEAPON X UNBOUND

WOLVERINE
WEAPON X UNBOUND

WRITERS
LARRY HAMA & FABIAN NICIEZA

PENCILERS
GERALD DECAIRE, MARC SILVESTRI, ANDY KUBERT & DARICK ROBERTSON

INKERS: **DON HUDSON, DAN GREEN & HILARY BARTA** WITH **TOM PALMER, KLAUS JANSON, AL MILGROM & JOSEF RUBINSTEIN**

COLORISTS: **GLYNIS OLIVER, STEVE BUCCELLATO & KELLY CORVESE** WITH **JOE ROSAS, KEVIN TINSLEY & MARIE JAVINS**

LETTERERS: **PAT BROSSEAU** WITH **MICHAEL HEISLER**

ASSISTANT EDITOR: **SUZANNE GAFFNEY** EDITOR: **BOB HARRAS**

FRONT COVER ARTISTS: **MARC SILVESTRI, DAN GREEN & VERONICA GANDINI**
BACK COVER ARTISTS: **MARC SILVESTRI & DAN GREEN**

COLLECTION EDITOR: **MARK D. BEAZLEY**
ASSOCIATE MANAGING EDITOR: **KATERI WOODY**
ASSOCIATE EDITOR: **SARAH BRUNSTAD**
ASSOCIATE MANAGER, DIGITAL ASSETS: **JOE HOCHSTEIN**
SENIOR EDITOR, SPECIAL PROJECTS: **JENNIFER GRÜNWALD**
VP PRODUCTION & SPECIAL PROJECTS: **JEFF YOUNGQUIST**
RESEARCH & LAYOUT: **JEPH YORK**
PRODUCTION: **COLORTEK, JERRON QUALITY COLOR & JOE FRONTIRRE**
SVP PRINT, SALES & MARKETING: **DAVID GABRIEL**

EDITOR IN CHIEF: **AXEL ALONSO**
CHIEF CREATIVE OFFICER: **JOE QUESADA**
PUBLISHER: **DAN BUCKLEY**
EXECUTIVE PRODUCER: **ALAN FINE**

WOLVERINE: WEAPON X UNBOUND. Contains material originally published in magazine form as WOLVERINE #47-57. First printing 2017. ISBN# 978-1-302-90388-6. Published by MARVEL WORLDWIDE, INC., a subsidiary of MARVEL ENTERTAINMENT, LLC. OFFICE OF PUBLICATION: 135 West 50th Street, New York, NY 10020. **Printed in the U.S.A.** ALAN FINE, President, Marvel Entertainment; DAN BUCKLEY, President, TV, Publishing & Brand Management; JOE QUESADA, Chief Creative Officer; TOM BREVOORT, SVP of Publishing; DAVID BOGART, SVP of Business Affairs & Operations, Publishing & Partnership; C.B. CEBULSKI, VP of Brand Management & Development, Asia; DAVID GABRIEL, SVP of Sales & Marketing, Publishing; JEFF YOUNGQUIST, VP of Production & Special Projects; DAN CARR, Executive Director of Publishing Technology; ALEX MORALES, Director of Publishing Operations; SUSAN CRESPI, Production Manager; STAN LEE, Chairman Emeritus. For information regarding advertising in Marvel Comics or on Marvel.com, please contact Vit DeBellis, Integrated Sales Manager, at vdebellis@marvel.com. For Marvel subscription inquiries, please call 888-511-5480. **Manufactured between 11/18/2016 and 12/26/2016 by LSC COMMUNICATIONS INC., SALEM, VA, USA.**

10 9 8 7 6 5 4 3 2 1

MARVEL® COMICS

WOLVERINE®

TM

$1.75 US
$2.15 CAN
47
OCT

02254

APPROVED BY THE COMICS CODE AUTHORITY

DIE YOUNG

STAN LEE PRESENTS:

DOG DAY

I TAKE IT YOU ARE THE *OWNER* OF THIS *MOTORCYCLE?*

GOT THE REGISTRATION IN MY POCKET, DARLIN'--

I'M NOT YOUR DARLING, BUB.

BUB.

THAT'S GOOD.

YOU DON'T THINK I'M RIPPIN' OFF THIS SCOOT, DO YOU?

NO, BUT I AM CURIOUS ABOUT WHY IT'S BEEN SITTING HERE CHAINED UP FOR *WEEKS...!*

LARRY HAMA SCRIPT
GERALD DECAIRE PENCILS
DON HUDSON INKS
PAT BROSSEAU LETTERING
GLYNIS OLIVER COLORING
BOB HARRAS EDITOR
TOM DEFALCO EDITOR IN CHIEF

... PARKING DOWN HERE AT THE WORLD TRADE CENTER IS AT A PREMIUM!
I WAS GOING TO HAVE IT CARTED OFF AND IMPOUNDED, BUT I RAN A CHECK ON THE TAG FIRST.
IT RAISED A FLAG IN THE COMPUTER AND BROUGHT DOWN ALL SORTS OF FEDERAL SECURITY TYPES ON MY CASE. SUIT AND HAIRCUT TYPES WITH S.H.I.E.L.D. I.D. CARDS AND A MOUTH FULL OF "NEED TO KNOW".
THEY SAID THEY WOULD APPRECIATE DISCRETION, BUT LEGALLY, IT WAS MY CALL.
I FIGURED I'D WAIT AND SEE JUST WHAT MISTER N.F.N. LOGAN LOOKED LIKE...
... AND HEAR WHAT KIND OF TALL TALE HE CAN SPIN AS I WRITE HIM UP!
M'AM, I WOULDN'T PRESUME TO PULL THE OL' FLIM-FLAM ON YOU...
... I COULD TELL YOU ALL ABOUT GETTIN' FLUSHED THROUGH THE SEWER SYSTEM, THROWIN' DOWN ON A PSYCHO-KILLER IN THE PARK, MESSIN' WITH AN INDIAN FOREST SPIRIT IN TIMES SQUARE, AND DUKIN' IT OUT WITH A GUY WHO THINKS HE'S MY FATHER AND A GAL WHO WANTS MY BONES --
-- BUT WHY SHOULD I HASSLE A NICE PERSON WHO'S JUST TRYIN' TO DO HER JOB?
JUST WRITE ME UP THAT TICKET AND I'LL BE ON MY WAY...
RRRIP!
WATCH WHERE YOU PARK NEXT TIME, MR. LOGAN.
KEEP THE BIG APPLE CLEAN

WESTCHESTER COUNTY. ONE TOWN OVER FROM SALEM CENTER.
TRACY!
WHAT ARE YOU DOING HERE? WE GOT A COURT ORDER--
WHATAYAMEAN WE, MOM? DAD'S BEEN PUSHING UP DAISIES FOR SIX MONTHS!
IT WAS YOU WHO KILLED HIM! HIS HEART COULDN'T TAKE THE STRAIN!
I TOLD HIM AFTER YOU DROPPED OUT OF THE VOLUNTARY PROGRAMS THAT THERE WAS JUST NO DEALING WITH YOU ANY LONGER, BUT HE WOULDN'T GIVE UP ON YOU!
YOU GOT ANYTHING AROUND HERE WORTH ANYTHING BESIDES THIS CHEAP JUNK?
HE WAS A CHUMP AND A SUCKER JUST LIKE YOU, MOM!
GET OUT OF HERE!
YOU'RE NOT STEALING ANYTHING ELSE FROM ME TO BUY DRUGS WITH!

YOU'RE NOT MY DARLING LITTLE TRACY-KINS ANY LONGER--!
--YOU'RE LIKE THE UNDEAD, COME BACK TO FEAST ON THE LIVING!
SOUNDS LIKE YOU'RE STILL READING THAT STEPHEN KING TRASH, MOM!
YOU'RE JUST BUGGED BECAUSE I'M NOT A CHUMP AND I'M NOT INTERESTED IN LIVING A STUPID BORING CHUMP LIFE AND--
--HEY! WHERE'D YA GET THAT? I COULD GET THREE OR FOUR YARDS FOR THAT ON THE STREET!
STAY AWAY FROM ME! I MEAN IT!
HAND IT OVER, MOM. YOU AIN'T SHOOTING ME AND YOU KNOW IT.
I WILL SO! I'LL-- I'LL WOUND YOU!
NEVAH HAPPEN, MOMSY!
GIVE IT OVER TO TRACY-KINS, MOMSY!

GOT IT!
PLEASE...!
WATCHOO GOT IN THIS THING?
HOO! HOT LOADS! BIG OL' MAGNUM HOLLOW POINTS!
MOMSY, YOU WAS LOADED FOR BEAR!
SOB WHAT DID I EVER DO TO DESERVE THIS...?
YOU WANNA KNOW, MOMSY-DOODLE? YOU REALLY WANNA KNOW?
YOU WERE A BORING, LAME CHUMP ALL YOUR BORING LAME CHUMP SUCKER LIFE!
ALL THE TIME, NAGGING, NAGGING, NAGGING!
FINISH SCHOOL! GET A HAIR-CUT! GO TO CHURCH! GET A JOB!
WELL, I GOT MYSELF A JOB, NOW!
IT'S A FULL TIME OCCUPATION!
IT'S CALLED GETTING STUPID!

ADAM-5, WE HAVE A REPORT OF A POSSIBLE **RABID DOG** AT THE CORNER OF ELM AND BATES--

DON'T LET HIM GET ANY CLOSER, JIM! SHOOT HIM AGAIN AND DON'T **MISS** THIS TIME!

YOU TAKE HIM OUT, DEIDRE! **YOU'RE** THE ONE WHO WINS ALL THE **SHOOTING TROPHIES**!

...BUT HE AIN'T SO FAR GONE THAT HE DON'T KNOW WHAT'S COMIN'.
INSIDE, BEHIND ALL THAT CRAZINESS, THERE'S SOMETHIN' WHIMPERIN' AND WAITIN' FOR THE PAIN TO STOP.
BLAM! BLAM! BLAM! BLAM!
THE DEPARTMENT MIGHT CALL THAT "EXCESSIVE FORCE".
I'VE GOT TWO LITTLE KIDS. I CAN'T AFFORD TO TAKE CHANCES.
YOU THINK THIS IS EASY?
I'VE GOT A DOG, TOO. I DON'T KNOW IF I COULD PUT DOWN SANDY MYSELF...
...YOU KNOW WHAT I MEAN? YOU HAVE A DOG, MISTER?
I HAD ONE...
...A LONG TIME AGO.

MOMSY WON'T BE DOING ANY DRIVING UNTIL SHE GETS OUT OF INTENSIVE CARE, SO I GUESS I GOT ME SOME WHEELS FOR A WHILE!
MIGHT AS WELL MAKE THIS A REAL "OLD HOME WEEK" KINDA DAY!
TRACY!
YO, MR. SINGH! THOUGHT I'D COME BACK AND SEE IF MAY-BE YOU GOT CANCER, SO I COULD SIT AROUND AND WATCH YOU DIE!
YOU GOT SOME NERVE, TRACY!
MR. SINGH GAVE YOU A JOB EVEN THOUGH HE KNEW YOU WERE FRESH OUT OF A DRUG REHAB PROGRAM AND YOU STILL ROBBED HIM, YA DEGENERATE DOPE FIEND!
YOU GET OUT OF MY STORE!
I AM TELLING YOU NEVER TO COME BACK!
GET OUTTA MY WAY, TIFFANY.
THESE STINKING FOREIGNERS COME OVER HERE, TAKE OVER EVERYTHING AND THINK THEY CAN GET AWAY WITH PAYING REAL AMERICANS COOLIE WAGES!
YOU'RE JUST A LOW-DOWN CRACKED-UP THIEF!
SHUT YER UGLY FACE, SKANK!
I'M JUST COLLECTING BACK PAY AND BENEFITS!

PUT THAT BACK, YOU--YOU-- BUMMER!
HEAR THAT? OL' SINGHAROO CAN'T EVEN GET OUR LANGUAGE STRAIGHT!

BLAM!
YOU SHOULDA LEARNT TO TALK ENGLISH RIGHT, SINGHY-BABY!

...BUT NOW, IT'S TOO LATE!

HOLY-- HAVE YOU GONE NUTS--?
OH NO! LORD, TRACY-- I DIDN'T MEAN TO SAY THAT--!
YOU'RE A SNIVELING LITTLE CHUMP, TIFFANY...
PLEASE DON'T SHOOT ME-- I SWEAR, I WON'T TELL--!
...YOU WERE CALLING ME A DEGENERATE, YA SKEEVY LITTLE ZIT-FARM?

CLICK!
NOOOOOOOOO!!!

WE HAD A DOG ONCE.

ME AND SILVER FOX.

DON'T WORRY, LOGAN. OLD BLUE WILL WANDER BACK ANY TIME NOW.

DOGS HAVE TO GO OFF BY THEMSELVES ONCE IN AWHILE. SOMETIMES THEY NEED TO BE WILD AGAIN...

IT'S BEEN A WEEK, SILVER FOX--

GRRRRRR!

HE'S GOT THE HYDRO-PHOBIA!
MUST'VE GOT BIT BY A RABID RACOON!

QUICKLY, LOGAN...!

...YOU HAVE TO PUT HIM DOWN!

SHOOT HIM, LOGAN...!

...SHOOT HIM!

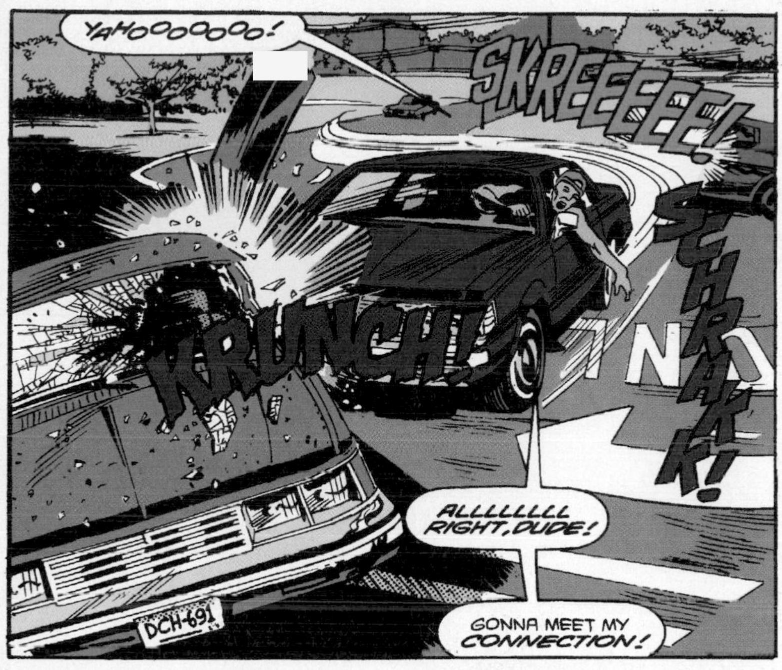
YAHOOOOOOOO!
SKREEEEEE!
KRUNCH!
SCHRAKK!
ALLLLLLLL RIGHT, DUDE!
GONNA MEET MY CONNECTION!
DCH-691

GONNA COP BIG TIME QUANITY!
GONNA GET SUPREMELY STUPID!
ALLLLLL RIGHT!

I'M FINALLY GETTING OVER!
HA! CHUMPS HAD BEST STAY OUT OF MY WAY!

THE LIGHT'S GREEN, MEGAN. THAT MEANS WE CAN CROSS.
MOM TOLD US TO LOOK BOTH WAYS FIRST, EVEN IF THE LIGHT IS GREEN, SEAN!
ARF!

OKAY!
NOTHING COMING FROM THE LEFT!
NOTHING FROM THE RIGHT!
LET'S GO, SANDY!

WOOOOOOO!
I AM SO LIT ALREADY...!
...IF MY MAIN MAN GOT SOME TRULY RIGHTEOUS TOTALLY FACE-WASTER MIND-ALTERING SUBSTANCES, I'M GONNA WARP OUT RIGHT THROUGH THE TRANSPORTER BAY!
OOOOOOOOOOH! BEAM ME UP, SCOTTY!
RUN, MEGAN!
SEAN--?
MY BIKE--!
VRROOOOM!
FORGET THE BIKE AND--
THINK FAST, KID!!

IS HE A COP?

HE'S GOT THAT LOOK.

THAT ATTITUDE.

LIKE HE DON'T TAKE NO GUFF.

IS HE CHECKING ME OUT?

DOES HE KNOW?

WHY DON'T THIS LIGHT CHANGE?

COME ON!

MOVE!

BRRRMM!

NOW, WHAT'S HE LOOKING AT?
THE KID'S BIKE HANDLE-BARS! THEY'RE STUCK ON MY GRILL!

HE KNOWS!
VROOOOOM!
...WELL, THAT'S JUST TOOOOO BAD!
HEY--!

SH-THOOOM!

THAT PUNK--
--HE'S STOPPIN'!

HE'S FLOORIN' IT IN REVERSE!!
VROOOOM!

WHOMP!
SREEEEEE!
GZAASH!
SNIKT!
SNIKT!
WHAT ARE YOU, ONE OF THOSE HALLOWEEN SLASHER GUYS WHO KEEPS POPPING BACK TO LIFE AFTER THEY BEEN CROAKED?
I GOT SOMETHING HERE TO PUT YOU DOWN FOR THE COUNT!

BLAM!
TZING!
LISTEN, KID--
--PUT DOWN THE GUN, AND LET'S TALK.
BLAM!
TALK? YOU GOTTA BE KIDDING?
I'M THE ONE WHO'S GOT THE .357 MAGNUM, CHUMP!
THOOP!
YEAH.
YOU GOT A BIG GUN, KID...
...BUT I GOT AN ADAMANTIUM-LACED SKELETON--
BLAM!
TWO FOR SINGH...
ONE FOR TIFFANY...
--HARDEST SUBSTANCE ON THE FACE O' THE PLANET.
THREE JUST NOW...
CLICK CLICK CLICK
I'M OUT OF AMMO!
ALSO GOT MY MUTANT HEALING FACTOR.

SNIKT!
DID YA RUN DOWN SOME LITTLE KID, BUB?
IS THAT HOW YOU GOT THEM HANDLE-BARS ON YOUR GRILL...?
...MOWED DOWN SOME POOR MOTHER'S DARLIN'
BY AND KEPT GHT ON DRIVIN' DOWN THE ROAD?
GNNNNG!
GRRRR!
HIM DOWN, LOGAN--!
WHERE'D ALL THAT CASH COME FROM? YOU BEEN REAL BUSY TODAY, BUB?
--YOU HAVE TO PUT HIM OUT OF HIS PAIN!
GRRRRR!
SNIKT!
SNIKT!

HOW WAS I SUPPOSED TO KNOW THAT?
HE WAS POINTING IT AT YOU. I MADE THE RIGHT DECISION.
I COULD HAVE--
ARF!
THAT *SLIME-BUCKET* ALMOST RAN DOWN MY *KIDS* AFTER HE BLEW AWAY TWO CIVILIANS AT A CONVENIENCE STORE!
CENTRAL? THIS IS *ADAM-FIVE*. WE HAVE SHOTS FIRED AND ONE PERP DOWN AT--

WHAT A DAY.

TWO MAD DOGS IN ONE AFTERNOON. TEN SHOTS FIRED. I'M GOING TO BE FILLING OUT PAPERWORK UNTIL--

--SAY, ARE YOU HURT?
NOTHIN' THAT WON'T HEAL BY ITSELF.
REMEMBER I TOLD YOU THAT I HAD A DOG ONCE?
YEAH.

HE CAME HOME FOAMIN' AT THE MOUTH. MY GIRL TOLD ME TO SHOOT HIM, BUT I COULDN'T DO IT...
...SO SHE TOOK THE RIFLE AND DID IT HERSELF.
END

MARVEL COMICS
WOLVERINE®
SHIVA SCENARIO PART 1
© 1991 MARVEL ENT GROUP INC
TM
$1.75 US
$2.15 CAN
48
NOV
UK 95p
APPROVED BY THE COMICS CODE AUTHORITY
BEGINNING: A QUEST INTO LOGAN'S PAST!
SILVESTRI + GREEN
30TH ANNIVERSARY
THE FANTASTIC FOUR 1961-1991
THE SEQUEL TO WEAPON X™
MEMORIES UNBOUND!

KEEP OUT
SNIKT!
ALBERTA, CANADA.

THE WILD AND WOOLY PART.
ZASH!

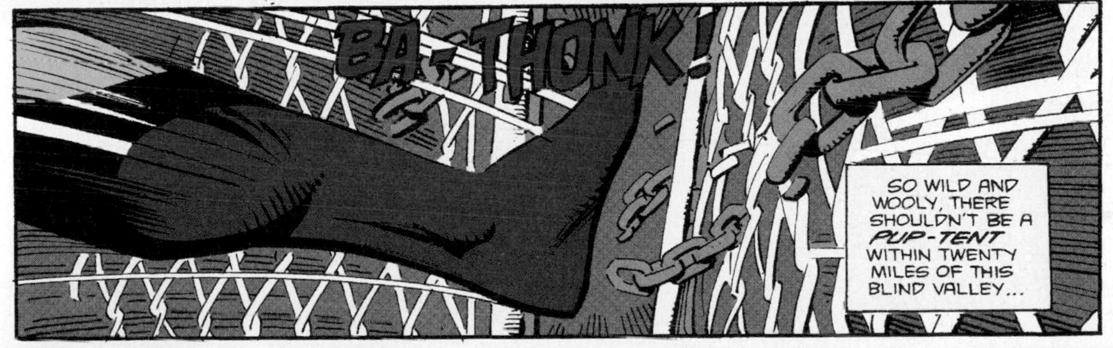
BA-THONK!
SO WILD AND WOOLY, THERE SHOULDN'T BE A PUP-TENT WITHIN TWENTY MILES OF THIS BLIND VALLEY...

...LET ALONE A BIG FENCED IN NUCLEAR RESEARCH FACILITY.

STAN LEE PRESENTS:
DREAMS OF GORE:
PHASE ONE
I'M GETTIN' CLOSE TO SOMETHIN' HERE.
THE SMELL O' THIS PLACE IS TICKLIN' MY MEMORY WAY DOWN DEEP.
I THINK I'VE BEEN HERE BEFORE...
...AND I DIDN'T LIKE IT.
YOU TWO COMIN' IN WITH ME?
YOU SURE IT'S SAFE TO GO POKING AROUND IN THERE, WOLVIE--?
KEEP
A TALE OF MEMORIES AND MYSTERIES BY:
LARRY HAMA...... SCRIPT
MARC SILVESTRI...... PENCILS
DAN GREEN...... INKS
PAT BROSSEAU...... LETTERING
STEVE BUCCELLATO...... COLORING
BOB HARRAS...... EDITOR
TOM DeFALCO...... EDITOR IN CHIEF

...I MEAN, I SURE DON'T WANT TO START GLOWING IN THE DARK OR DEVELOPING ANY WEIRD NEW TALENTS!
YOU GOIN' CHICKEN ON ME, JUBE? THIS PLACE HAS BEEN ABANDON-ED FOR YEARS.
RADIATION STICKS AROUND FOR CENTURIES, WOLVIE!
AHH, THE PUZZLE-PALACE SPOOKS HANG NUKE-WARNIN'S ON ANY FACILITY THAT THEY DON'T WANT THE PUBLIC PEEKIN' INTO.
GET OL' HARRY TABESHAW TO HOLD YER HAND.
THIS IS AS FAR AS I GO. HATE TO TROT OUT A MOLDY CLICHE, BUT THAT PLACE IS BAD MEDICINE.
HEAR THAT, WOLVIE? OUR GUIDE SAYS IT'S A NO-NO!
YOU DIDN'T BLINK TWICE WHEN RONALD PARVENUE HIRED YOU TO TRACK DOWN THE HUNTER IN DARKNESS FOR HIM.
I THOUGHT YOU DIDN'T BELIEVE IN STUFF LIKE FOREST SPIRITS, TABE-SHAW?
I DON'T, BUT I DO BELIEVE IN BEING CAREFUL.
I BACK-TRACKED ALL THE HUNTER'S LAIRS TO THIS PLACE THAT ISN'T EVEN ON THE SURVEY MAPS. OTHER ANIMALS HAD TAKEN OVER THE OLD LAIRS EVEN THOUGH THEY HAD A STRONG PREDATOR SCENT...
...BUT THIS PLACE, THIS IS SOMETHING ELSE.
NOT A SINGLE ANIMAL EVER GOES NEAR THIS PLACE. NOT AN OWL, A SNAKE NOR A MOUSE.
THINK ABOUT THAT.

ARE YOU THINKING ABOUT THAT, WOLVIE?
NOT MUCH.
YOU COMIN' OR NOT?
GIMME A SEC' TO LACE UP! I FINALLY GOT SOME *HARDTOP* TO PRACTICE ON!

HMMM...STEEL REINFORCED CONCRETE BUILDINGS WITH NO WINDOWS.
GOVERNMENT PROPERTY - NO - TRESPASSING
SOLID STEEL DOORS.
LIKE THIS PLACE WAS DESIGNED TO KEEP SOMETHING HEAVY FROM GETTING OUT...

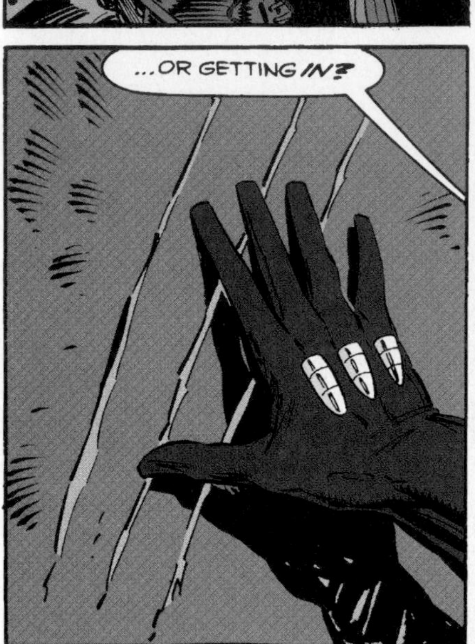

...OR GETTING *IN*?

WHEEEEEE!
I BET YOU THOUGHT I WAS *NUTS* TO DRAG THESE *BLADES* ALONG ON A WILDERNESS TREK, HUH?
DON'T BE SKATIN' DOWN NO RABBIT HOLES, NOW...

DON'T *WORRY!* I'M GETTING TO BE A REGULAR *TAI BABILONIA* ON THESE THINGS--
--*HEY!* CHECK THIS *OUT!!!*
FIND SOMETHIN', JUBILEE?

YEAH! A WHOLE BIG MACADAM PARKING LOT!
JUST MORE SKATIN' SUR-FACES?
SURE, BUT WHERE THERE'S A PARKING LOT IN AN INDUSTRIAL COMPLEX...

...THERE'S GOTTA BE LOADING BAYS AND GARAGE DOORS!
I WAS HERE...
I WAS HERE AND I DON'T REMEMBER ANY OF IT.

I WAS TRYING TO GET INSIDE AND SOMEBODY WAS SHOOTING AT ME FROM IN THERE.
IF I COULDN'T CLAW MY WAY THROUGH BACK THEN--
TRY THE HANDLE!

IT HAS TO BE LOCKED--
NOT NECESSARILY!

HOW ABOUT THAT?
OOOOOH! LOOKIT THAT CAR! WHAT IS IT, WOLVIE?

A *LOTUS SEVEN.*
NEVER HEARD OF IT.
HOW'D YOU KNOW WHAT IT WAS?
JUST *KNEW.*

HUNH! WELL, THERE'S GOTTA BE A DOOR THAT LEADS INSIDE THE COMPLEX FROM HERE!
YOU GO LOOK FOR IT, DARLIN'...
...I'VE GOT STUFF TO ATTEND TO RIGHT HERE.
FEELS LIKE THE SEAT'S ADJUSTED JUST FOR ME...
NEXT TO MIRACULOUS IF THE ENGINE TURNS OVER--
SKOFF
VRAUVRAAA!
MR. LOGAN?

COLD.
HOW DID IT GET SO COLD?
PHUP!
THAT SHOULD DO IT. GET HIM OUT OF THERE.
THAT INTRA-MUSCULAR THORAZINE WORKS FAST.
SOME-BODY HAS TO MOVE THE LOTUS.
AFTER WE MOVE HIM.
UHF.
HELP ME WITH HIM.
YUH.
HE'S REAL HEAVY FOR JUST...
...A LITTLE GUY...
TOK!

DIDN'T YOU GET HIM WITH THAT STUPID STUN GUN?
COURSE I DID!
POINT BLANK!
UNNNGH!
SPRACK!
GOT HIM!
DO HIM, QUICK!
USE THE STUN GUN AGAIN!
I'LL STUN HIM ALRIGHT--

THAT'S THE WRONG END YOU'RE USING!
NOT AS FAR AS THIS LUG IS CONCERNED!
PROF'S NOT GONNA LIKE THIS!
HE SAID NO BODY DAMAGE!
VOK!
SURE!--
BUT HE DIDN'T SAY WHAT A TOUGH SON-OF-A-GUN HE'D BE!
WELL, NOBODY'S SO FULL OF TOUGH THAT IT CAN'T BE PISTOL-WHIPPED OUT OF HIM.
THAT'S A FACT.
WHUMPP!

YOU DON'T LOOK SO HOT, WOLVIE...

...MAYBE YOU SHOULD GIVE UP THOSE CIGARS AND TAKE UP BLADE-SKATING?

JUST HAVIN' SOME SORT O' CRAZY DAY-DREAM.
COULDN'T BE A FRAGMENT O' REAL MEMORY...

IT WAS TOO--
I FOUND A DOOR BACK THERE. IT'S LIKE ALL COVERED WITH CLAW MARKS BUT IT'S UNLOCKED...

WHAT'S THE DEAL WITH THIS CAR?
I THINK IT USED TO BE MINE.
WOW! YOU USED TO HAVE GOOD TASTE!
MAYBE THE REGISTRATION IS STILL IN THE GLOVE COMPARTMENT--

YOU FIND ANY SOUVENIRS FROM SOME HOT DATES IN THERE, YOU JUST LEAVE 'EM BE.
I FIND ANY PANTIES, I'M NOT TOUCHING THEM.
I WAS THINKIN' O' GRENADES, DARLIN'.
LOOKS LIKE SOMEBODY LIT OFF A FEW FRAGS IN HERE...
...AS WELL AS A FEW THOUSAND ROUNDS O' MILITARY BALL AMMO.
THAT MUCH FIRE-POWER IN AN ENCLOSED SPACE.
THEY MUST'VE BEEN DESPERATE--
WHAT WERE THEY SHOOTING AT?
WHAT OR--
--WHO?
--OUT OF CONTROL!
AWOOOOOOOOGAA!

WEAPON X HAS ESCAPED!
WE HAVE AN UNTENABLE SITUATION HERE IN ZONE 3!
WHERE'S THE PROF--?
AWOOOOOGA
--WHY ISN'T HE DOWN HERE WITH-- AKKK!
ZONE 3, RESPOND IF YOU CAN!
SKAK!
ZONE 3 IS TOTALLY COMPROMISED!
GET SOME WRANGLERS DOWN THERE!
SCHRRECK!
WRANGLERS? WHAT WE NEED ARE HEAVY WEAPONS TEAMS AND SAPPERS!
WE HAVE AN INFRARED SENSOR ALARM IN THE CRAWL-SPACE--SECTION 17!
MOVEMENT?
...RUNNING AMOK, YOU MIGHT SAY.
DEFINITELY HEADED TOWARDS THE PROF'S QUARTERS!
THE PROFESSOR IS LOCKED UP IN THERE AND HE'S NOT ANSWERING!
CLEARING THE DEAD WOOD AS YOU PUT IT.
SERVES THAT BALD-HEADED SON-OF-A--

KRAACH!
YAAAAARGH!
AAAAH HELP MEEE!!
MOVE IT!
ZONE THREE AND C-BLOCK!
NONONONONONONO!!!
WEAPON X IS IN THERE WITH THE PROF!
DOOR'S LOCKED! BRING UP THE ENGINEER!
C-4 AND PRIMACORD ON THE HINGES! GO! GO!
YO! LOOKIT WHAT I FOUND!
AHHHHHHH!
HEY!
CHILL OUT...!

JUBILEE!
ARE YOU NUTS--?
YOU KNOW HOW CLOSE YOU CAME TO--
NUTS? MOI?
YOU'RE THE ONE STANDING AROUND IN A DARK CORRIDOR GRUNTING AND BREATHING HEAVY!
GET A GRIP!
HERE.
FOUND THIS IN THE LOTUS.
YOU MUST HAVE BEEN A REGULAR JAMES BOND!
WHY IS THE HANDLE ALL TAPED UP--?
BETTER GRIP. NO FINGER-PRINTS.
IT'S MY BACK-UP PIECE.
IF YOU'RE GONNA INSIST ON PACKIN' THAT REGULATION PEA-SHOOTER YOU MIGHT AS WELL HAVE TWO OF 'EM!
YOU FIGGER THIS JOB IS THAT HAIRY?
THEY'RE ALL HAIRY FAR AS I'M CONCERNED.
YOU READY?
LET'S DO IT.
CLICK!

YOU GOT SOME ROTTEN LUCK, PARTNER--
CATCHIN' A JOB LIKE THIS ON YOUR BIRTHDAY!
I REALLY FEEL FOR YA!
YEAH?
SO WHERE'S MY CAKE?
YOU WANT CAKE? IN WINDSOR, YOU WANT CAKE?
AFTER THIS I'LL TAKE YOU NORTH, 'CROSS THE RIVER, TO DETROIT. GREEK-TOWN. GET SOME BACLAVA!
THIS IS IT.
LEMME RAISE THE "OUTSIDE MAN".
SQUEEEE!
LET'S GET THIS OVER WITH. I WANNA GET BACK TO THE HOTEL IN TIME FOR THE "AVENGERS."
3G
"MASTODON," THIS IS "SABRETOOTH." READY WHEN YOU ARE.
TIME TO ROCK AND ROLL, PARTNER!
YOU'RE THE DESIGNATED KICKER, "SABRETOOTH."
TAKE IT DOWN.

PSYCH. OUT
EVERY-BODY FREEZE!
KA-THUNK!
WE'RE BUSTED!
STATE
HANDS UP! MOVE IT!
GRENADES
RPG-7
ROCKET LAUNCH
XPLOSIVE
YOU SAID THE PIGS COULDN'T COME ACROSS THE BORDER, ANDRE!
SOME PIGS THINK THINK THEY HAVE A SPECIAL DISPENSA-TION!
RATATATATAT!
I'LL DISPENSATE THEIR FUNKY BUTTS--
BLAM! BLAM! BLAM!
AAAAA!
I'LL GET HIM!
THWUMP!
BLAMM!
MORSE!
BA-DOOOM!

MASTODON! WHERE THE HECK ARE YOU? WOLVERINE IS DOWN!
WHUMP!
UHHHHH...
HURTS SO BAD.
DEAD.
NO! NOT DEAD!
ANIMAL!
NO! LOGAN!
IT IS CRUCIAL THAT THE MEMORY IMPLANT BE BONDED TO REALITY...
HURTHURTHURTHURT
...PREFERABLY TO SEVERE TRAUMA.
HIT THE DECK, SABRE-TOOTH! I'M COMING THROUGH!
BEHIND YOU, CARLISLE! ANOTHER PIG!
BIG MAN WITH A SAWED-OFF, HUH?
KRASH!
HOW YOU LIKE IT IN THE GUT?
BA-DOOM!
UNNGGH
BA-DAM!
...H-HOW DO YOU LIKE IT IN THE F-FACE?

BRRRRRRIIIP! CLUNK!
THRRIP!
JAMMED!
GET HIM, SILVER-FOX!
GAAAAAH!
YA LITTLE FOUR-EYED--
S-S-SILVER-FOX?
I'M HIT, LOGAN--!
THE BRAIN DOES NOT ALLOW ITSELF TO REMEMBER EXCRUCIATING PAIN IN PRECISE DETAIL.
BLAM!
CLICK!
I'M EMPTY!
GET IT TOGETHER, LOGAN--!
--OR WE'RE ALL DEAD MEAT!
THESE ARE APPROPRIATE "GREY AREAS" TO BUILD ON, TO LAYER IN "ALTERNATE SCENARIOS"...
BLOW HIM AWAY, YOU STUPID SQUAW!
MORSE HAS GOT A DEATH-GRIP ON THIS GUN! GOTTA BREAK HIS FINGERS--
EXPLOSIVE
SNAP! POP!
NEVER MIND! I GOT MY GUN UNJAMMED!
DIE PIGS!

NOT PIG!
NOT ANIMAL!!
NOT DEAD!!
THP!
THUD!
THOOP!
BLAM! BLAM! BLAM! BLAM!
GUHHHH!
BRRIPP!
PONK!
THE REAL TRICK TO GIVING THE IMPLANT CREDENCE LIES IN ARTFUL JUXTAPOSITION...
PIG! STINKIN' RUNNIN' DOG FASCIST PIG!
YOU JUST BLEW AWAY A TRUE REVOLUTIONARY AND A CERTIFIED GENIUS!
AARRCH!
THE BRAIN WOULD MUCH RATHER BELIEVE AN UNPLEASANT FICTION THAN A HORRIFYING TRUTH. THE IMPLANT OVERPOWERS REALITY BY BEING MAR- GINALLY MORE PALATABLE.
YOU'RE DEAD!!
IT'S ALL IN THE PLACEMENT, YOU SEE.

NOT ANIMAL...
NOT DEAD...
...L-L-LOGAN!
D-DROP GUN...
NOT BEAST... WON'T HURT...
NO!
HUMAN! HUMAN!!
SHE SAID "NO!", LOGAN! DO HER!
SCHRRAK!
THE GIRL, LOGAN! YA GOTTA NEUTRALIZE THE GIRL!
GO AHEAD, PIG! I'M NOT GOING TO GROVEL FOR MY LIFE--
I SEE THE SUBJECT'S MEMORY AS A COMPLEX RAGOUT, AND WE ARE THE CHEFS...
...WHO HAVE IT WITHIN THEIR POWER TO DETERMINE WHAT SHALL RISE TO THE TOP AND WHAT SHALL BE SKIMMED.
YOW!

I WAS JUST HOLDING OUT THE KEYS TO THE LOTUS, WOLVIE!
YOU DIDN'T HAVE TO STICK ME!
SORRY, JUBE.
LOOKS LIKE YOU GOT A BIG OLD PAD-LOCK KEY ON THERE, TOO.
WHAT'S THE POUCH?
LOOKS INDIAN...
GOTTA GET OUT O' THIS PLACE, JUBE.
IT'S JARRIN' LOOSE TOO MANY QUESTIONS...
QUESTIONS I GOTTA ASK XAVIER ABOUT.
02 SHIVA
WE'RE HEADIN' BACK TO WEST-CHESTER, DARLIN'.
DON'T YOU EVEN WANT TO CHECK OUT WHAT'S IN THE REST OF THIS PLACE?
I'VE SEEN ENOUGH.
02 SHIVA
NEXT MONTH: THE ANSWERS BEGIN!

MARVEL COMICS
WOLVERINE
SHIVA SCENARIO PART 2
© 1991 MARVEL ENT GROUP INC
GUEST-STARRING JEAN GREY AND PROFESSOR X
$1.75 US
$2.15 CAN
49
DEC
02254
APPROVED BY THE COMICS CODE AUTHORITY
THE JOURNEY CONTINUES!
...IF MY LIFE BE A LIE!

1407 GRAYMALKIN LANE, SALEM CENTER, NEW YORK...
...OSTENSIBLY, THE XAVIER SCHOOL FOR GIFTED YOUNGSTERS--
--BUT IN ACTUALITY, THE HEAD-QUARTERS OF A SECRET BAND OF MUTANTS KNOWN AS THE X-MEN WHERE THREE OF THAT NUMBER HAVE GATHERED TO SOLVE A DECADES-OLD MYSTERY.
...SO WHEN IS THIS PROCEDURE GOIN' TO BEGIN?
I DON'T MIND ANY OF THE DANGERS YOU WARNED ME ABOUT AS LONG AS THIS MIND-PROBE CAN REALLY UNLOCK SOME O' THE SECRETS ABOUT MY PAST!
PROFESSOR XAVIER! HE ISN'T EVEN AWARE--
OF COURSE NOT, JEAN. IN ORDER FOR THE PROCEDURE TO WORK, THE APPARENT CONTINUITY MUST BE SEAMLESS.
YOU'RE LOSIN' ME, PROF. WHAT'S HE MEAN, JEAN DARLIN'?
YOU'RE ALREADY INTO THE MIND-PROBE, WOLVERINE...
NO WAY.
HEY. I NEVER SAW THAT DOOR BEFORE--
DREAMS OF GORE: PHASE 2
(REMEMBERANCE? OF THINGS PAST?)
LARRY HAMA--SCRIPT MARC SILVESTRI--PENCILS GREEN/BARTA--INKS PAT BROSSEAU--LETTERING STEVE BUCCELLATO--COLORING BOB HARRAS--EDITOR TOM DeFALCO--EDITOR IN CHIEF
THE TRANSITION FROM ACTUAL REALITY TO THE PERCEPTUAL REALITY TO THE MEMORY MATRIX IS IMPERCEPTIBLE, LOGAN...

...YOU ARE "WALKING" THROUGH A GALLERY OF MEMORY ICONS CONSTRUCTED IN YOUR OWN MIND BY MYSELF AND JEAN. THEY MARK THE PATHWAYS THAT MAY LEAD YOU TO THE SYMBOLIC DOORS...
...BEHIND WHICH LURK THE REPRESSED MEMORIES YOU SEEK.
GOOD LUCK, AND GOOD HUNTING!
WHAT'S GOIN' ON?
BRAIN FEELS LIKE IT'S BEEN SHOT FULL O' NOVOCAINE!
EARS RINGIN' LIKE QUASIMODO'S HANGOUT!
THE PAIN!
EVERYTHING'S
TURNIN'
RED!!!
GRRR RRR
SNIKT!
SNIKT!
DOZEN BODY SHOTS--NO EFFECT!
THIS IS A MASSACRE!
FALL BACK! FALL BACK!

SECURITY AT ZONE THREE! I WANT A SITUATION REPORT!
WHAT IS THE CONTAINMENT FEASIBILITY FOR WEAPON X?
CONTAINMENT FEASIBILITY?
NOTHING SHORT OF A TACTICAL NUKE IS GOING TO TAKE OUT THIS WACKO!
HE MUST BE STOPPED! YOU HAVE YOUR ORDERS!
NOOOOO!!!!
THIS IS NOT REAL!
NOT TIME DIS-PLACEMENT!
JUST MEMORY!
I'M HERE
TO
FIND
SOMETHING!

NOT TO RELIVE THE PAST!
IF THIS REALLY IS MY PAST!
CAN'T LET MYSELF SLIP BACK...
...INTO MINDLESS BERSERKER STATE.
HAVE TO TAKE CONTROL.
TOO MUCH TO FIND OUT.
WHAT DID XAVIER SAY?
THESE DAYS OF PAIN...
...AND KILLING!
HE SEVERED A STRUCTURAL SUPPORT STRUT!!!
SYMBOLIC DOORS?
THIS ONE'S SOLID AS A BANK VAULT.

NOT EVEN ADAMANTIUM CLAWS ARE GONNA SLICE THROUGH THIS--
SHIVA
NO ACCESS
WITHOUT
CLEARANCE
TAP
TAP
TAP
HUH?
THUD THUD THUD
SECURITY GOONS--!
THERE YOU ARE...!
...I'VE BEEN SCOURING HALF O' THE SIERRA MAESTRA LOOKIN' FOR YOU!
NOBODY TELLS US NOTHIN' OUT HERE IN THE BOONIES!
I JUST GOT WORD FROM HAVANA! PRESIDENT KENNEDY'S BEEN SHOT! IT HAPPENED TWO DAYS AGO AND I JUST FOUND OUT!
FOLLOW ME, PARTNER! I KNOW A CANTINA WHERE THEY GOT A TV SET!
PROBABLY THE ONLY TV IN THE WHOLE TOWN O' PALMA SORIANO!
SABRETOOTH!

WRONG CODE-NAME! I'M EL TIGRE ON THIS OPERATION!
AND MY CODE-NAME...?
EMILIO...
...EMILIO GARRA.
<...THIS IS THE CUBAN PEOPLE'S NEWS SERVICE WITH THE LATEST UPDATE ON THE SO-CALLED ASSASSINATION IN DALLAS OF THE CRIMINAL KENNEDY-->*
<TWO DAYS AGO? THIS IS NOVEMBER 24, 1963?>
<--THE ACCUSED GUNMAN LEE HARVEY OSWALD IS NOW BEING TRANSFERRED FROM THE DALLAS POLICE HEADQUARTERS TO-->
<THEY REALLY DID IT! THEY WENT AHEAD AND DID IT! AND THEY GOT A RED HERRING TO TAKE THE FALL!>
<OSWALD DIDN'T PULL THE TRIGGER?>
YOU'RE JOKING, RIGHT?
YOU KNOW WHAT THIS MEANS?
NOW IT'S OUR TURN! WE GOTTA DO OUR JOB!
WE GOTTA--
BLAM!
*TRANSLATED FROM SPANISH.

THAT REALLY TEARS IT!
C'MON, COMPADRE-- WE GOTTA GO TO WORK!
COOL IT, JULIO. YOU'RE MOUTHIN' OFF IN INGLES!
<THERE THEY ARE!>
<THE TWO YANQUI SPIES THAT INDIO INFORMER TOLD US ABOUT!...>
<...EL TIGRE AND GARRA!>
<SHOOT THEM!!>
WE'VE BEEN BLOWN!
BLAM! POW!
I KNEW IT! THAT TWO-FACED MESTIZA SOLD US OUT!
ZORA DEL PLATA, THE LITTLE FOX OF THE SIERRAS!
BA-DAMM!
HE CALLED US YANKS! DOESN'T HE KNOW WE'RE CANADIANS?
CANUCKS?!? YOU'RE A REAL BUNDLE O' LAUGHS TODAY, PARTNER!
YOU TAKE A STRATEGIC WITHDRAWAL THROUGH THE BACK DOOR WHEN I POP UP AND HOSE 'EM DOWN WITH THE THOMPSON GUN!

GO FOR IT! TRY TO MAKE IT TO GITMO!
YOU KNOW THE EXTRACTION POINT!
THE BACK DOOR...
RATATATATATAT!
...WHERE DOES IT REALLY LEAD TO?
WHATEVER THIS IS, IT SURE AIN'T A BACK-ALLEY IN THE SLUMS O' PALMA SORIANO.
LOOKS LIKE THE SORT O' PLACE A FELLA COULD RUN INTO ROD SERLING IN.
HIM, OR THE CRYPT-KEEPER.
SOME O' THESE DOORS LOOK LIKE THEY'RE FROM MANSIONS, AND SOME LOOK LIKE THEY'RE FROM...
...LOG CABINS.
LORD.
THE MEMORY COMES FLASHIN' BACK LIKE SUN-LIGHT THROUGH THE CLOUDS...
LOGAN + SILVERFOX
IT WAS SPRINGTIME WHEN I CARVED THAT.
SPRINGTIME FOR ME AND SILVER FOX.
CARVED IT WITH MY FATHER'S OLD KNIFE--
MY FA--
WHY WON'T THE REST OF THAT MEMORY COME THROUGH?
WHAT'S BEHIND THIS DOOR???
CREEEEEEAK!

NOTHIN'.
NOTHIN'!!!
BAFF!
PROFESSOR XAVIER! JEAN!
THAT BLANK DOOR IS A MANIFESTATION OF BLOCKS DELIBERATELY PUT INTO YOUR MEMORY.
CERTAIN DATA HAS BEEN SEALED OFF. SOME OF WHAT YOU PERCEIVE TO BE REAL MEMORIES MAY VERY WELL BE ARTIFICIAL IMPLANTS WITH HIDDEN TRIGGERS.
DON'T GIVE IN MINDLESS GESTURES, WOLVERINE...
THIS IS GETTING TOO DANGEROUS--
SLAMM!
WHAT ARE YOU GETTIN' AT?
HE'S TRYING TO TELL YOU TO BACK OFF. YOUR MEMORY HAS BEEN TAMPERED WITH BY EXPERTS AND THEY'VE SET TRAPS THROUGHOUT YOUR MIND.
OPEN A FEW TOO MANY WRONG DOORS AND THE DAMAGE COULD BE IMMENSE. YOU MIGHT FIND YOURSELF REVERTING TO...TO...
WHAT? I COULD BECOME AN ANIMAL AGAIN, JEAN? ISN'T THAT SOMETHING THAT DOESN'T KNOW WHERE IT CAME FROM? SAME DIFFERENCE.
THIS COULD REALLY HURT YOU, LOGAN--
PAIN AND ME ARE OLD BUDDIES.
I GOTTA SEE THIS OUT...

NO?
IS THAT "NO, I DON'T KNOW" OR "NO, I AIN'T TELLIN'"?
THAT VOICE.
SABRE-TOOTH.
THIS PLACE...
...I REMEMBER IT NOW. IT'S ACROSS THE RIVER.
WINDSOR, ONTARIO.
ME, SABRETOOTH, AND MASTODON WERE ON AN OP--
THAT'S "NO, I WOULDN'T TELL YOU WHERE THE FAUCET WAS IF YOUR FACE WAS ON FIRE!"
NO! NO! NO! NOOOOO!
WHAPP!
DON'T TELL ME, "NO", YA NASTY LITTLE SQUAW!
BACK OFF, SABRETOOTH!
JUST LET HER BE!
CRUNCH!

WHAT?
YOU WANT SOME O' THIS ACTION?
BE MY GUEST, PARD. I GOTTA GO CALL THE "CLEANERS"...
...CAN'T BE HAVIN' THE LOCAL GENDARMERIE STUMBLE OVER OUR HANDIWORK EVEN IF WE HAVE AN UNDER-THE-TABLE AGREEMENT WITH OTTAWA.
LET'S GO, MASTODON --THE GIRL'S CUFFED TIGHT AND HER PALS ARE DEADER'N TROTSKY!
WHOA. BACK UP HALF A SEC... DIDN'T WE ALL GET SHOT FULL O' HOLES IN THIS CLUSTER-FOUL UP?
HRMPH!
THAT'S WHY WE WEAR THE BULLET-PROOF VESTS, SPORT!
ALL YA GOTTA WORRY ABOUT IS STOPPIN' A SLUG WITH YOUR FACE!
THAT COULD ONLY HELP A MUG LIKE LOGAN --I MEAN, WOLVERINE'S, HUH?
SNAP! POP!
LET'S GET SCARCE, MASTO-DON...
...WE WANNA GIVE THE LITTLE HAIRY FIREPLUG PLENTY O' TIME TO "INTERROGATE" THE PRISONER!
HA HA HA HA HA HA!

DON'T YOU KNOW ME, SILVER FOX?
SURE.
I KNOW YOU...
...YOU'RE LOGAN.
YOU REMEMBER?
YOU REALLY REMEMBER?
SURE I DO!
COME HERE, BABY!
OH, DARLIN'...
IS THIS MEMORY REAL?
THEN THAT TERRIBLE THING THAT HAPPENED AT THE CABIN WAS A LIE!
THIS MUST BE THE TRUTH.
THE SMELL OF HER HAIR...
THE TOUCH OF HER FINGERS...

DO YOU REMEMBER OUR CABIN?
SURE I DO, HON.
DO YOU REMEMBER IT IN WINTER, WITH THE ICICLES HANGING FROM THE EAVES?
YEAH. IT LOOKED LIKE A PICTURE IN A CALENDAR...
SCENIC, WILD AND BEAUTIFUL ALBERTA
WE HAD A DOG. OLD BLUE.
ONE DAY HE CAME HOME, FOAMIN' AT THE MOUTH AND I HAD TO... YOU HAD TO...
DO YOU REMEMBER WHAT HAPPENED ON MY BIRTHDAY?
THAT COULDN'T HAVE HAPPENED, BECAUSE THIS IS YEARS LATER AND YOU'RE STILL ALIVE--
--THAT'S RIGHT, PIG...!
...AND YOU'RE DEAD!
CLICK! CLICK! CLICK!
I EMPTIED BOTH GUNS INTO THE PROFESSOR OVER THERE. DO YOU REMEMBER THAT?
THE PRO-FES-SOR...?

...THAT'S ANDRE.
WHO'S THE PROFESSOR?
SAME GUY. HE'S LYIN' IN THAT POOL O' BLOOD NEXT TO THAT--
--CALENDAR.
THAT'S IT! THAT'S OUR CABIN!
SCENIC, WILD AND BEAUTIFUL ALBERTA
IS THIS SOME KIND O' CRUEL JOKE?
AM I SUPPOSED TO BELIEVE THAT THE TINY SHREDS O' HAPPY MEMORIES I HAVE ARE BASED ON A CHEAP CALENDAR PAINTING?
IT DON'T WASH!
I REMEMBER!
SCENIC, WILD AND BEAUTIFUL ALBERTA
I REMEMBER THE WAY THE LATE AFTERNOON SUN TURNED THE INSIDE BRIGHT ORANGE AND BROUGHT OUT RED HIGHLIGHTS IN YOUR HAIR...
YOU DON'T REMEMBER ANY OF THIS, DO YOU?
LOOK, THIS ISN'T FUNNY ANY-MORE. WHAT ARE YOU, SOME KINDA WACKO?
YOU'RE ONE OF THOSE IM-PLANTS.
YOU'RE NOTHING BUT SMOKE.
SNIKT!
I'D RATHER TAKE MY CHANCES WITH THAT SABRE-TOOTH CREEP! YOU'RE A LOONY-TOON!
IS THIS ALL FAKE? WHAT WILL I FIND BE-HIND THESE WALLS ...?
SCHRECK!

...NOTHING ??????
THIS ROOM, THE TENEMENT BUILDING-- THIS IS JUST A STAGE SET COBBLED TOGETHER OUT O' MAGAZINE CLIPPIN'S AND SOMEBODY ELSE'S IMAGINATION?
SOME O' WHAT I REMEMBER HAS GOT TO BE REAL!
AS REAL AS THIS NUMBNESS SPREADIN' THROUGH MY BRAIN ...
MY TEETH SO HOT THEY BURN MY TONGUE.
AS REAL AS THIS RED HAZE IN FRONT O' MY EYES.
NOW IT'S MY BONES. THEY'RE BURNIN' UP!
THE HEAT.
THE PAIN.
THE FIRE INSIDE.
WHITE HOT THORNS POKIN' THROUGH A WORLD O' ICE...
SILVER FOX!
SHOW ME--
NO! DON'T TAKE HER AWAY!
SHE HAS TO SHOW ME THE TRUTH--!
SHOW ME!!!

SHOW.
ME.
SHOW ME THAT LATEST READ-OUT, HINES.
IT LOOKS POSITIVE, PROFESSOR. SOLID IMPRINT WITH NEGLIGIBLE RESIDUAL MEMORY LEAKAGE.
FADE IN THREAT-SCENT OVERLAY FROM TRACK FOUR.
READINGS?
HEARTRATE STEADY. RESPIRATION NORMAL. ALPHA IS OFF THE GRAPH--!
SILVER FOX?
ARE YOU IN THERE?
YEAH, BUT WHAT'S HE SEEING?
SHLUCK!
SILVER FOX?
...DIRECT INPUT INTO ALL SENSORY CENTERS AT FULL LEVEL. HE'S HAD THE SCENT AND THE AUDITORY, NOW HE'S GOT THE VISUAL.

HE SEES THE BEAR. ALL THE SENSORY INPUT ADDS UP TO IT.
ADRENAL RISE WITH CARPAL FLUX.
DOES HE SEE THE BEAR THE WAY WE WANT HIM TO SEE IT?
WE FEED HIM AN INFRARED TARGETING SCAN. KEEPS HIM OFF BALANCE. JACKS UP THE STRESS.
--AND ENHANCES THE ILLUSION OF OUTSIDE CONTROL.
WE HAVE FULL CLAW EXTRUSION.
HE'S GOING FOR IT!
GOOD SOLID STRIKE!
DO WE HAVE A TAKE ON THAT? CAN WE JUICE UP THE KILLING STIMULUS AND LOCK IT? WE HAVE THE TSI STANDING BY?
AFFIRMATIVE. THIS IS IT. THIS IS OUR SWITCH. ONCE WE LOCK IT IN WITH THE TSI, WE CAN TURN ON WEAPON X AT WILL...

HOW ABOUT TURNING HIM OFF?
THAT'S WHAT SHIVA IS FOR.
SHOW ME ...
...SHOW ME!
STAND BY. WE HAVE TRAUMATIC SHOCK IMPRINT READY ON THE FADER.
NO WAY!
I'M NOT BUYING THIS ONE!
LEVEL'S TOO LOW. NOT IMPRINTING.
FEED IN THE BACK-UPS.
WHAT HAPPENED TO THE BEAR??
PLURAL. ALL OF THEM?
THAT'S SUPPOSED TO BE ME, HUH?
IS THIS SUPPOSED TO SCARE ME?
PILE ON THE TRAUMA. JACK UP THE FEAR CENTER. WE NEED AN IMPRINT...

PUSH THE ENVELOPE. HE HAS A HIGH PAIN THRESHOLD.
"TAKES A LICKIN' AND KEEPS ON TICKIN'."
COME ON!
...YOU THROW DOWN ON ME, I'LL PUT YOU IN A WORLD O' HURT!
WRONG TACK. PHYSICAL TRAUMA WON'T WORK.
I DON'T CARE IF YOU'RE IMPLANTS, OR FIGMENTS' OR YESTERDAY'S PIZZA...
RIGHT. WHAT HAVE WE GOT ON MENTAL ANGUISH? THE GIRL AGAIN... OR THE FATHER?
BRING HIM BACK. I DON'T CARE WHAT HE SAID, THIS IS TOO MUCH.
IT'LL TAKE A FEW SECONDS TO KICK IN, JEAN...
JEAN...
HUH?
JEAN?
HE SHOULD BE COMING OUT OF IT...

...RIGHT ABOUT NOW!
PLEASE MAKE A NOTE, JEAN--HE REQUIRED TEN TIMES THE NORMAL DOSAGE.
QUICKLY, DO YOU KNOW WHO YOU ARE?
...LOGAN.
WOLVERINE.
WHO AM I, AND WHERE ARE WE?
YOU'RE PROFESSOR XAVIER AND WE'RE IN THE X-MANSION...
...IN THE PSI-LAB.
WHAT USED TO BE THE PSI-LAB.
UNFORTUNATELY, OUR RESTRAINTS WERE NOT ADAMANTIUM!
YOU BROUGHT ME BACK TOO SOON!
I WAS JUST ABOUT TO FIND OUT MORE ABOUT SILVER FOX AND MORE ABOUT MY FATHER--
OH, LOGAN--DON'T BLAME HIM. I MADE HIM STOP IT...
...I COULDN'T STAND TO SEE YOU THAT WAY--
I NEED TO KNOW.
JEAN'S JUDGEMENT WAS ENTIRELY EMOTIONAL, BUT MINE WAS WHOLLY RATIONAL. I THINK IF WE HAD ALLOWED YOU TO CONTINUE, YOU WOULD HAVE GONE OVER THE EDGE INTO UTTER MADNESS.
AS IT IS, THERE WAS PROBABLY CONSIDERABLE DAMAGE RESULTING IN A POSSIBLE REVERSION TO A MORE ... ANTI-SOCIAL STATE.

NO WAY.
I DON'T FEEL ANY DIFFERENT-- TAKE YOUR HANDS OFF ME, DARLIN'.
YOU SAYIN' I COULD BE- COME AN ANIMAL AGAIN?
THERE IS THE DISTINCT--
I'LL NEVER BE AN ANIMAL AGAIN!
I'M LOGAN!
I'M HUMAN!
NOT AN ANIMAL!
NOT A WOLVERINE!
YOU CAN'T JUST STOP BEING WHAT YOU ARE...
I'M AN X-MAN!!
NOT AN ANIMAL!
LOGAN--
GOTTA GET OUTTA HERE.
GOTTA GET SOME AIR.

THE NUMBER YOU HAVE DIALED IS A LIMITED ACCESS SECURE LINE. AFTER THE TONE, PLEASE ENTER YOUR PERSONAL IDENTIFICATION NUMBER. *BEEEEEEEP!*

CLICK! DEPARTMENT OF AGRICULTURE, PEST CONTROL SECTION. HOW MAY WE HELP YOU?

I WOULD LIKE TO ORDER TWENTY SEVEN COPIES OF YOUR PAMPHLET, "KNOW THE SEVENTEEN YEAR LOCUST".

TELEPHONE

GAS

SET YOUR SCRAMBLER TO 349 AND HOLD.

BZZZT! YOUR SAFE LINE IS CLEAR. YOU MAY PROCEED.

HELLO?

HELLO. THIS IS *HINES.* IS THAT *YOU,* SIR?

JUST GET ON WITH IT.

WE'VE BEEN TRACKING HIM EVER SINCE HE SET OFF THE DETECTORS UP IN *CANADA* BUT HE'S BEEN IN THAT *PLACE* IN WESTCHESTER. CAN'T GET TOO CLOSE...

MARVEL® COMICS

TM

CODENAME: WOLVERINE®

TOP SECRET

WEAPON X FILE

$2.50 US
$2.95 CAN
50
JAN
02254

APPROVED BY THE COMICS CODE AUTHORITY

PRIORITY CLEARANCE
ONLY
NOT TO BE SEEN
BY MAJOR LOGAN

Japan
His Imper
Hir
Emperor
Requests
at the wedding
Lady Mariko
of Clan Yashida
to Logan
Hey Elf- don't forget the BEER! -W.
R.S.V.P.
XAVIER'S SCHOOL
FOR GIFTED YOUNGSTERS
MUTATIS MUTANDIS
AMERICAN EXPRES
AIR CANADA
499:212
FLIGHT 277
DESTINATION
LOGAN
MARC + DAN-
Princess Bar

WEAPON X
BIOMOLECULAR ADAMANTIUM SYNTH
ETABOLIC VARIABLE SKELETAL ADAPTATIO
SHIVA SCENARIO
PART 3
75.102
.005
42.001
77.008
112.405
77.101
167.501
.E.L.D.
Beaver
ATHABASCA
WOOD BUFFALO NATIONAL PARK
Little Smoky
ATHABASCA
O'chiese Indian Preserve
Red
Gull Lake
ALBERTA
WILLINGDON
Logan
United States of America
CENTRAL INTELLIGENCE AGENCY
LOGAN
SECRET SERVICE
CANADA
CANADIAN SECRET SERVICE

STAN LEE PRESENTS THE 50TH ISSUE OF WOLVERINE!
DREAMS OF GORE: PHASE 3
UNANSWERED QUESTIONS.
THAT'S WHAT I'VE GOT PLENTY OF.
HECK, MOST OF MY PAST IS AN UNANSWERED QUESTION.
HEY!
JUST WHO DO YOU THINK YOU ARE, BUSTER?
DARLIN', IF I KNEW THE ANSWER TO THAT QUESTION...
SCRIPT: LETHAL LARRY HAMA
PENCILS: MURDEROUS MARC SILVESTRI
INKS: DANGEROUS DAN GREEN
WITH HELP FROM HILARY BARTA AND TOM PALMER
COLORING: STOMPIN' STEVE BUCCELLATO
LETTERING: PUNISHIN' PAT BROSSEAU
EDITOR: BRUTAL BOB HARRAS
EDITOR IN CHIEF: TERRIBLE TOM DeFALCO

...I WOULDN'T BE HERE!
YOW!
SOMEBODY GET HIS LICENSE NUMBER!
GONNA SUE ME?
I'M WARNIN' YOU...
...MY LAWYER'S A PSYCHOTIC MUTANT.
HRMPH!
IS THAT A REDUN-DANCY, OR WHAT?
HOLD THAT ELEVATOR!
THE REST O' YOU, GET OUTTA THE WAY!
BEST STEP BACK, DARLIN'--
SKREEEE
--DON'T WANT THEM LONG LEGS BRUSHIN' UP AGAINST THE HOT TAIL-PIPE, DO YOU?
WANNA HIT THE TOP FLOOR BUTTON FOR ME?
THIS IS SECURITY SEVEN. HE'S COMING UP IN ELEVATOR #3, BUT HE'S GOING TO HAVE TO TRANSFER TO A FREIGHT...
...THE PASSENGER CARS DON'T GO ALL THE WAY TO THE ROOF!

THEN.
FORGE, SINCE YOU'RE MR. KNOW-IT-ALL AROUND HERE...
WHAT DO YOU WANT TO KNOW, WOLVERINE?
THE S.H.I.E.L.D. HELI-CARRIER. HOW DO THEY RE-SUPPLY THAT THING?
NOW.
20
IT'S AGAINST THE LAW TO SMOKE THAT NASTY CIGAR IN HERE AND YOU REALLY SHOULD BE TAKING THAT GREASY MACHINE UP IN THE FREIGHT ELE-VATOR.

MOSTLY, IT'S AIR-LIFTED BY BIG TRANS-PORTS, EXCEPT FOR THE WATER AND JET FUEL. THAT THING HAS THREE REACTORS AND A SQUADRON OF JP-4 GUZZLING FIGHTERS. DO THE MATH.
THEY USUALLY PIPE BOTH ABOARD AT NIGHT FROM SHIPS AT SEA. BUT SINCE THE MIDDLE EAST BROUHAHA DI-VERTED HALF THE FLEET, THEY'VE BEEN RESUPPLYING FROM A COVERT URBAN SITE.
40
THE CIGAR AIN'T LIT, THE SCOOT AIN'T GREASY, AND THE FREIGHT AIN'T MY CUP O' TEA...
WHY DO YOU ASK?

YEAH.
IT'S THE TOP OF THE CITICORPS BUILDING IN MID-TOWN MANHATTAN.
YOU GOING TO FRONTAL ASSAULT THE S.H.I.E.L.D. HELICARRIER WITH YOUR MOTOR-CYCLE?
THEN.
NOW.
COLONEL FURY, SIR?
WE SEEM TO HAVE A CONTROLLABLE COMPROMISE IN THE SECURITY ENVELOPE--
ARE YOU TRYIN' TO TELL ME THAT SOME HAIRY MUTANT GAVE THE GUARDS THE SLIP? YOU THINK THROWIN' IN THAT WORD "CONTROLLABLE" WILL MITIGATE MY ATTITUDE ABOUT THIS CLUSTER FOUL-UP, LIEUTENANT?
SIR, I AM PREPARED TO TAKE FULL RESPONSIBILITY--
THEN YA BETTER GET YOUR YOUNG KEISTER IN GEAR AND UN-COMPROMISE THAT SECURITY ENVELOPE! AM I MAKIN' MYSELF CLEAR?
THEN.
YEP.
THAT'S EXACTLY WHAT I'M PLANNIN' TO DO.

HEY, LIEUTENANT, HEARD THE COLONEL CHEW YOU OUT. DON'T SWEAT IT! WE'VE GOT THE FREIGHT ELEVATOR COVERED!
IT'S OPENING--!
--EMPTY!
BUT WHERE --?
THEY SAID HE WAS ON A MOTORCYCLE! THIS IS THE ONLY WAY HE COULD GET UP HERE, UNLESS--
BUMP BUMP BUMP BU
VRROOOMMMMM!
--HE TOOK THE STAIRS!
I ALWAYS KNEW THAT WATCHING THOSE EVEL KNEIVEL SPECIALS WOULD COME IN HANDY SOME DAY.
A REAL WEALTH O' PRACTICAL INFORMATION.

...THIS ERSTWHILE INTRUDER IS GOING TO SPLATTER LIKE A BUG ON A WINDSHIELD!

YA EVER HEAR OF *ADAMANTIUM,* LIEUTENANT?

SCHRECK

NICHOLAS, I GOT A BONE TO PICK WITH YOU...
I'LL BET YA DO, LOGAN.
BUT HOW'RE YOU GONNA KEEP ALL THESE HIGHLY MOTIVATED YOUNG TURKS FROM THROWIN' DOWN ON YOU LIKE A MONTH OF SUNDAYS?
YOU'RE GONNA TELL 'EM TO LAY OFF.
NOW, WHY WOULD I DO THAT?
'CAUSE THE DIRECTOR O' CENTRAL INTELLIGENCE IS GONNA WANT YOU TO. THE MAN'S GOT A LOTTA JUICE.
WHY--
'CAUSE, YOU'RE GONNA GET ON THE DIRECT LINE TO HIM...
...AND TELL HIM THAT I KNOW ALL ABOUT EL TIGRE AND EMILIO GARRA AND WHAT THEY WERE DOIN' IN CUBA IN 1963 AND MAYBE-- JUST MAYBE--
--HE SHOULD THINK TWICE ABOUT LETTIN' THE OL' CANUCKLE-HEAD READ HIS OWN SECURITY DOSSIER!
I SUPPOSE IF ANYTHING HAPPENS TO YOU, A LETTER GETS DROPPED OFF AT THE DAILY BUGLE?
NATCH.
MIGHT TAKE A WHILE.
YA GOT TEN MINUTES.

NINE MINUTES LATER...
YER FILE'S COMIN' THROUGH ON THE FAX, LOGAN. YOU LIKE WALKIN' THE RAZOR'S EDGE, DON'CHA?
HOW ELSE YOU GONNA KNOW YOU'RE ALIVE?
WOW!
CHECK THIS OUT!
A FLAG JUST WENT UP ON OUR MONITORING SCANNER DOWN IN MARYLAND--
--YOU KNOW THAT PROGRAM WE RUN THAT PICKS OUT THE ANOMALIES IN THE RETRIEVAL SYSTEM OF THE NATIONAL SECURITY AGENCY'S COMPUTER BANKS? IT JUST PAID OFF IN SPADES!
VERY GOOD, PARSONS. I HAD BETTER SHOW THESE TO THE BOSS.
THESE ARE S.H.I.E.L.D. FILES THAT HAVEN'T BEEN PULLED FOR OVER TWENTY YEARS...
WAS THIS THE ONLY HARD COPY, PARSONS?
YES, SIR.
ERASE ALL RECORDS OF THIS IN OUR SYSTEM.

ENTER.
NOK!
AHEM.
...OUR PENETRATION OF THE NSA COMPUTER SYSTEM HAS YIELDED A CLASS THREE ANOMALY.
THE DCI USED HIS PRIORITY CODE TO PULL A SET OF RECORDS THAT HAVE BEEN DORMANT FOR TWO DECADES.
THE CROSS-REFERENCE SENT UP A FLAG IN OUR MONITORING SYSTEM...
...A FLAG YOU PERSONALLY WROTE INTO THE PROGRAM ON OCTOBER 5, 1972. THE FLAG ACTIVATOR IS THE NAME "LOGAN"--
I AM PERFECTLY CAPABLE OF REMEMBERING MY OWN ACTIONS.
DID OUR PENETRATION DEVICE DETECT ANYBODY ELSE FLAGGING AND MONITORING THIS FILE AND CROSS-REFERENCES?
OUR HIGH IMPENDENCE MONITOR TRACED A DATA FLOW TO ANOTHER SYSTEM THAT MATCHES THE FILE VOLUME EXACTLY.
IT'S A DESK-TOP SYSTEM AT THE DEPARTMENT OF AGRICULTURE IN WASHINGTON D.C...
...THE PEST CONTROL SECTION OF ALL PLACES.
GO BACK TO YOUR DESK.
AS YOU COMMAND.

THE NEXT DAY, IN WASHINGTON, D.C...
WHO DO YOU THINK YOU ARE? YOU CAN'T JUST BARGE IN WITHOUT AN APPOINT-MENT! THIS IS THE UNITED STATES DEPARTMENT OF AGRICULTURE--!
--I AIN'T HERE TO LOBBY FOR SOYBEAN SUBSIDIES, I JUST WANNA JAW WITH THE BALD-HEADED PROFESSOR-GUY WHO'S THE DIRECTOR O' THE PEST CONTROL SECTION.
YOU KNOW, SKINNY FELLA WITH RIMLESS SPECS...
NO SUCH PERSON, NO SUCH SECTION, AND GET YOUR KNUCKLES OFF MY DESK!
IZZATSO?
THEN THE FILE I GOT FROM THE NSA MUST BE WRONG!
I GUESS THIS PEST CONTROL SECTION WAS NEVER SET UP TWENTY YEARS AGO AS A FRONT FOR A REAL NASTY DIRTY TRICKS PROJECT!
I GUESS THAT GUY I SMELL COWERIN' BEHIND THIS DOOR COULDN'T POSSIBLY BE THE PRO-FESSOR, SOMETIMES KNOWN AS "ANDRE" IN MY DREAMS.
GET AWAY FROM THAT DOOR! AND IF YOU'RE THINKING OF FORCE, YOU SHOULD KNOW THAT THERE'S STEEL PLATE UNDER THE WOOD VENEER!
YOU EVER HEAR OF ADAMANTIUM, LADY?
ASK THE PROFESSOR. HE KNOWS ALL ABOUT IT.
SNIKT! SCHLUNK!

IF I WANT TO GO ONE-ON-ONE WITH THE PROF...
...THIS SISSY LIL' DOOR AIN'T STOPPIN' ME.
SCHLICK!
I'M GONNA NAIL HIM, BUT I'M GONNA DO IT LEGAL...
...WITH ALL THE HARD EVIDENCE I'M GONNA TRACK DOWN, STARTIN' WITH THAT WAREHOUSE UP IN WINDSOR, ONTARIO!
AND YOU CAN TELL HIS PAL, HINES--
--THAT IF SHE WANTS TO TAIL THE OL' HAIRY MUTANT, SHE'S GOTTA STAY DOWN-WIND!
GOOD LORD!
D-DID YOU HEAR THAT?
NOT EVEN SHIVA CAN STOP HIM!
TERMINATION PARAMETERS FOR PROJECT X
STOP THAT GIBBERING, HINES. WE HAVE WORK TO DO!

THAT AFTERNOON...
THE NSA FAXED YOU THIS ENTIRE FILE, WOLVERINE? THERE ARE OVER FIFTY THOUSAND PAGES OF DOCUMENTATION AND AN EQUAL NUMBER OF PHOTOGRAPHS, DIAGRAMS, CHARTS, MAPS AND EKG PRINTOUTS!
AFTER THE FIRST HUNDRED PAGES I HAD 'EM RUN OFF FLOPPY DISKS THROUGH THE MODEM--TOOK TWO SHOE-BOXES FULL O' DISKS...
THAT CERTAINLY MAKES THEM EASIER TO WORK WITH.
DON'T YOU THINK YOU'RE BEING A BIT PRECIPITOUS--ZOOMING UP TO CANADA BEFORE WE'VE EVEN HAD TIME TO SIFT THROUGH THIS MASS OF DATA, PROPERLY?
I READ ENOUGH TO KNOW THERE'S PRECIOUS LITTLE IN THAT FILE ABOUT MY PERSONAL PAST. REAMS O' STUFF ABOUT PROJECT X AN' HOW IT WAS A CIA OP SHELTERED IN CANADA THROUGH A COVERT DEAL...
WE'RE PASSING THE WAYPOINT AT CHAUTAUQUA LAKE, JEAN.
GOT IT MARKED, CYCLOPS. CHANGING HEADING TO 270 DEGREES MAGNETIC AND BEGINNING DESCENT...
...I DID FIND THAT COPY OF THE WAREHOUSE LEASE IN WINDSOR. SET UP THROUGH A DUMMY CROP DISEASE RESEARCH GROUP THAT GETS ITS FUNDING FROM THE PEST CONTROL SECTION!
COINCIDENCE? WHY DO I HAVE THIS CRAZY MEMORY O' WINDSOR STARRIN' SILVER FOX, SABRETOOTH AND A CAST O' TERRORISTS?
A PARTICULARLY VIVID DREAM, PERHAPS?
NO WAY, I WALKED THROUGH THAT PLACE. I KNOW IT.
LOOK AT YOU, LOGAN. THE COSTUME CHANGE... YOUR VERY MANNERISMS! IT'S AS IF YOU'RE REVERTING TO THE MAN THE X-MEN FIRST MET YEARS AGO. AND THAT FRIGHTENS ME.
PROFESSOR XAVIER, WE ARE MAKING THE FINAL APPROACH TO THE TARGET IN ULTRA STEALTH MODE...

...AND RE-VECTORING THRUSTERS FOR VTOL.
THE WAREHOUSE IS RIGHT BELOW US, LOGAN.
WOLVIE--?
CAN I--?
YOU CAN'T COME WITH ME, JUBILEE. THIS IS SOMETHIN' I GOTTA DO BY MYSELF.
BUT--
XAVIER AND JEAN ARE RIGHT THERE AND IF THEY CAN'T TELL IF SOMETHIN'S GONE WRONG, I'M IN MORE TROUBLE THAN I CAN GET OUT O' WITH YOUR HELP...
HE BROUGHT HIS FRIENDS WITH HIM...!
...YOU SAID HE'D COME ALONE!
THEY WERE SIMPLY TRANSPORT, HINES...
...HE WON'T TAKE THEM DOWN INTO HIS MURKY PAST WITH HIM!
THE PEST CONTROL PEOPLE HAVE ARRIVED. THEY ARE MAINTAINING A SURVEILLANCE FROM THE ADJACENT ROOF...
JUST AS I EXPECTED.
KEEP TRACK OF BOTH PARTIES.
AS YOU COMMAND!
ALL HAIL HYDRA!
YES, YES-- HAIL AND ALL THAT!

LIGHTS.
BACKDROPS.
SALOON
#22 HOTEL ROOM
#62 SENIOR PROM
THIS WHOLE FLOOR IS A BIG SOUND-STAGE.

EVERYTHIN' YOU NEED TO MAKE MOVIES IS HERE...
TERRORIST HIDEOUT

...EXCEPT THE CAMERAS!

IS THAT WHAT MY PAST IS?
ZASH!
A CHEAP MOVIE?

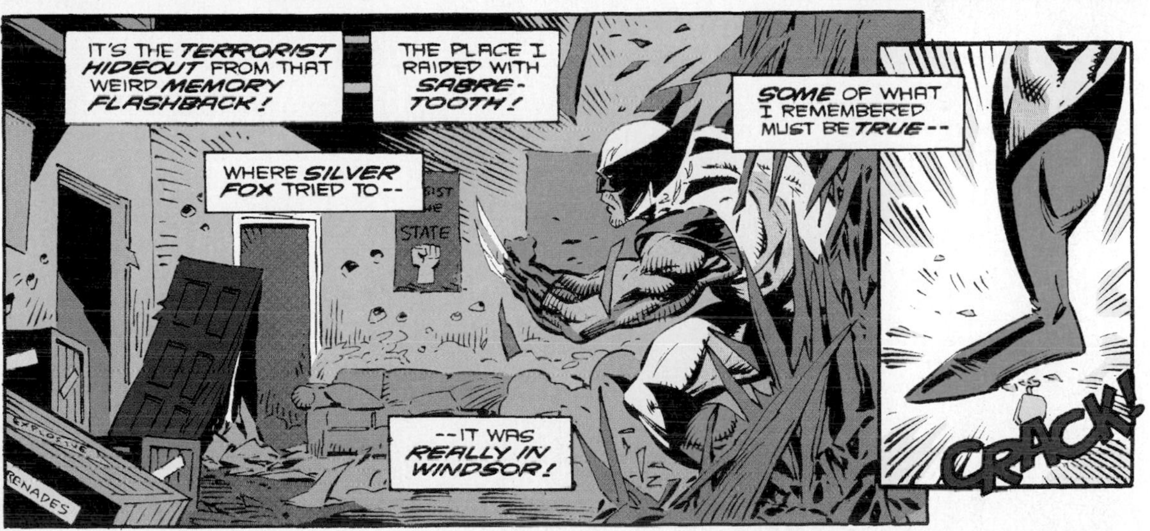
IT'S THE TERRORIST HIDEOUT FROM THAT WEIRD MEMORY FLASHBACK!
THE PLACE I RAIDED WITH SABRE-TOOTH!
WHERE SILVER FOX TRIED TO--
SOME OF WHAT I REMEMBERED MUST BE TRUE--
--IT WAS REALLY IN WINDSOR!
STATE
CRACK!

GLASSES.
ANDRE'S GLASSES.
THE PROFESSOR'S GLASSES.
WHOSE--
--SOMETHIN' DIFFERENT HERE!
SAN FRANCISCO NEWSPAPERS AND FLIERS...
TONIGHT AT THE FILMORE
THE GRATEFUL DEAD
NOVEMBER
...AND THAT CALENDAR!
WHAT HAPPENED TO THE PICTURE OF THE CABIN??
SCENIC CASTROVILLE CALIFORNIA
ARTICHOKE CAPITAL OF THE WORLD!!
HOME OF THE GIANT! ARTICHOKE!
THERE WAS A CALENDAR PICTURE OF THE CABIN I LIVED IN WITH SILVER FOX--
I OPENED MY EYES AFTER I HIT THE FLOOR AND THIS CALENDAR WAS RIGHT IN MY FACE.
I WAS STARIN' AT THE CABIN WHEN MASTODON CAME CRASHIN' IN THROUGH THAT WINDOW WITH THE WIND BLOWIN' IN BEHIND HIM OFF THE RIVER--
--NO!
#244 TERRORIST HIDEOUT
WHAT'S GOIN' ON HERE?
THIS PLACE WASN'T IN SAN FRANCISCO!

WHOSE MEMORIES ARE THESE, ANYWAY?
BACKWOODS SALOON
SCHRACK!
THE SALOON.
WENT EYEBROWS TO KNUCKLES WITH SABRETOOTH FOR THE FIRST TIME IN HERE.*
ALL THE WAY I REMEMBER IT...
...DOWN TO THAT SLICE O' CAKE WITH THE PINK FROSTIN'.
*SEE ISSUE #10.

SCRACK!
A SAWMILL.
SOMEBODY WITH CLAWS HAD A KNOCK-DOWN DRAG-OUT TO BEAT THE BAND IN HERE...
...BUT I SURE DON'T REMEMBER IT.

ZRECK!
A SENIOR PROM I KNOW I NEVER WENT TO.
THIS REALLY TEARS IT.
SENIOR PROM
HOW MANY OF US WERE HERE GETTIN' OUR MEMORIES SCRAMBLED IN THIS JOINT?
FOR WHAT REASON?

SCHRACK!
SOMEBODY'S LIVIN' ROOM!
NEVER SAW IT BEFORE!
ZZREK!
COMPUTER LAB.
DOESN'T RING ANY BELLS.
POK!
SHUKK!
I CAN REMEMBER EVERY JUNGLE I EVER BEEN IN...
...AND THIS AIN'T ONE O' THEM.
SPAK!
THAT'S IT.
CHECKED 'EM ALL OUT AND THE ONE I WAS DREADIN' FINDIN' WASN'T THERE!
NO CABIN-- THAT LITTLE PLACE IN THE WOODS WHERE I LIVED WITH SILVER FOX...
...THERE'S A CHANCE THAT THE ONE SHININ' GOLDEN TIME IN MY LIFE WAS REAL!

I JUST PICKED UP A MIND-BLAST OF THE MOST PURE AND UTTER HAPPINESS FROM WOLVERINE...
WE NEEDN'T DIVERT PRECIOUS ENERGIES TO MONITORING HIS STATE OF MIND...

...WHEN WE HAVE MEGA-BYTES OF DATA TO SIFT THROUGH, MOST OF WHICH IS EXCEEDINGLY BANAL TRIVIAL NONSENSE.
GOSH, I'M BORED ALREADY!
FORGE WROTE UP A BUNCH OF NEW PROGRAMS TO ANALYZE THE DATA...
--THEY SET UP COMPARISON FIELDS, MATCH NUMBERS, LIST ANOMALIES AND RUN FLAG SEARCHES. WITH ENOUGH HANDS ON THE KEYBOARDS, THIS MAY NOT TAKE AS LONG AS WE FEARED...

I DON'T EVEN LIKE STARING AT A COMPUTER SCREEN IF MARIO IS RUNNING ACROSS IT IN HIS RACOON SUIT!
IF WOLVIE IS HAVING SUCH A GREAT TIME DOWN THERE, WHY ARE WE STUCK UP HERE WITHOUT EVEN AN IN-FLIGHT MOVIE?

THOSE TURTLES HAVE A PIZZA-WARMER IN THEIR VAN. YOU'D THINK WE'D HAVE AT LEAST A SLUSHY MACHINE--
THAT'S ENOUGH--
--SIT DOWN AND START CRUNCHING NUMBERS AND LISTS!

...THAT ALL THE SUBJECTS OF THE PROJECT HAVE OVERLAPPING FALSE MEMORIES?

YOU ARE ASCRIBING POWERS OF DEDUCTION TO THIS SUBJECT THAT ARE OUT OF PROPORTION TO HIS KNOWN CAPACITIES.

GOOD. THE CENTRAL COMMAND CENTER SEEMS TO BE INTACT. LET'S HOPE THE TUBES HAVEN'T BURNED OUT IN THE LOW-LIGHT SURVEILLANCE CAMERAS.

WHY A COMMAND CENTER? I THOUGHT SHIVA WAS SELF-ACTIVATING.

HE IS.

BUT WE THOUGHT IT BEST TO HAVE SOME OPTIONS AVAILABLE AFTER ACTIVATION.

SHUNK!

CANCEL RESET DEFAULT

HAS HE FOUND SHIVA YET?

HE HASN'T EVEN STUMBLED ON THE RANDOM INTRUDER ELIMINATOR YET...

AIN'T THIS SOMETHIN'!
THE OL' CANUCKLE-HEAD FALLS FOR THE OL' "TRAP-DOOR IN THE STAIRS" BIT--
FRACK!
--AND GOES TUMBLIN' DOWN THE OL' RABBIT-HOLE...
SNIKT!
...ONLY IT'S A SURE BET THAT THERE AIN'T NO WONDER-LAND AT THE BOTTOM O' THIS SHAFT!
SNIKT!
SHUNK!
NOPE.
JUST A WORLD O' HURT.
WHAT'S AT THE BOTTOM O' THOSE STAIRS THAT SOMEBODY DON'T WANT ANYBODY TO SEE THIS BAD?
AIN'T THAT A KICK IN THE HEAD!
IT'S SOMETHIN' I'VE SEEN BEFORE...

I SAW THIS *VAULT DOOR* IN THAT *DREAM-TRIP* I TOOK THROUGH MY OWN SUPPRESSED *MEMORIES...*

...BUT IT WAS AT THE *PROJECT X COMPLEX!*

SHIVA NO ACCESS WITHOUT CLEARANCE

WHAT'S IT DOIN' *HERE?*

SSSSSSSSSSS
"...IT'S A SHAME REALLY, TO TERMINATE THIS SUBJECT.
WHA?
WHO ARE YOU--?
THOOM!
I AM SHIVA...
...I AM THE DESTROYER!

IZZAT SUPPOSED TO IMPRESS ME, BUB?
BECAUSE IT SURE DON'T!
SNIKT!
SNIKT!
SCHRACK!
C'MON, BUB--
--LESSEE YOU DO SOME DESTROYIN'!
SKRRANG!
OH, MY!
JUST A TEMPORARY SETBACK, HINES.
NOW, WE SHALL SEE WHAT SHIVA IS ALL ABOUT!
SHUK!

...PUT A FANCY SUIT ON AN ANDROID AND HE THINKS HE'S HOT STUFF.
THAT AN AXIOM?
SHOULD BE.
PROFESSOR XAVIER! LOOK AT WHAT SHOWED UP IN THE LAST SORT!
AMAZING!
THIS IS THE VERY PROPOSAL FOR THE WEAPON X PROGRAM...!
...ITS PURPOSE, TO CREATE A POOL OF SUPER-SOLDIERS, AWARENESS OF THEIR OWN POWERS SELECTIVELY MIND-WIPED FROM THEIR MEMORIES!
THE CANDIDATES WERE THEN WARE-HOUSED IN THE GEN-ERAL POPULATION UN-TIL THEY WERE NEEDED AND THEN REACTI-VATED AND CONTROLLED!
WHERE DID THE MUTATIONS COME FROM? DID THEY--?
PROFESSOR, LOOK AT THIS MEMO ABOUT SUPRESSION OF AGING FACTORS!
I AM SHIVA!
I AM THE DESTROYER!
SHIVA IS THE PROGRAM.
THE KILLER ROBOT IS JUST ITS TOOL.
AND SHIVA LEARNS FROM HIS MISTAKES...
...YOU CAN'T FOOL HIM THE SAME WAY TWICE!

PULLED YERSELF BACK TOGETHER, HUH, BUB?

I HAVE MY *SOUND-DAMPERS* ON--YOU HAVE BEEN UP-GRADED WITH *INFRARED DETECTORS*, LOGAN?

NAH, I CAN *SMELL* THE *SOLDER* ON YOUR HOT *CIRCUIT BOARDS*--

--YOU KNOW MY *NAME*--!

THWAMMM!

OF COURSE I DO.

YOU ARE MY *PRIMARY TARGET*...

THOOOM!

...YOU ARE *FIRST* ON MY *LIST*!

SSCHUKKK!

I FOUND A LIST!
WOLVERINE
SABRETOOTH
FOX
KESTREL
VOLE
AND LOOKIT WHO'S ON IT!
WHY IS WOLVERINE'S THE FIRST NAME?
BECAUSE HE'S EXCEL-LENT!
THAT MAY BE, JUBILEE-- BUT IT MIGHT ALSO BE PRIORI-TIZATION--
--AND IF SO, FOR WHAT?
...THAT WHICH THE PROJECT CREATES, THE PROJECT MUST BE ABLE TO DESTROY!
THE SCALES MUST BALANCE!
ORDER MUST BE RESTORED!
SSSSSHHOOOOOOOOOOOMM!
I HAD YOU PEGGED FOR A NEATNESS FREAK--
--IF YOU WASN'T A ROBOT, I'D SAY IT WAS LOUSY POTTY-TRAINING!
I DON'T UNDERSTAND... YOU CAN JUST ORDER UP ANOTHER ONE EVERY TIME ONE GETS DE-STROYED?
DON'T BE RIDICULOUS! WE HAD A LIMITED BUDGET! WE HAVE A FINITE NUMBER OF BACK-UPS, BUT THEY ARE QUITE SUFFICIENT...

"...BESIDES, SHIVA IS A DEDICATED PROGRAM. HE HAS A HIDDEN ACE. HE IS ARMED WITH THE TRIGGERS!"
I PUT YOU THROUGH THE CHOP-SHOP ONCE AND I GUESS IT DIDN'T STICK...
...THIS TIME I'M MAKIN' SURE THAT NONE O' THE KING'S HORSES PUT YOU BACK TOGETHER AGAIN!
PATHETIC AND PREDICTABLE.
SSTHOOOM!
...AFTER ALL, WE WERE PUTTING PERFECT KILLING MACHINES BACK INTO THE GENERAL POPULATION.
WE NEEDED A FAIL-SAFE...!
YOU LEAD WITH THE LEFT AND FOLLOW UP WITH A RIGHT UPPERCUT.
SSSSSS
CAN YOU SURVIVE YOUR MISTAKES LONG ENOUGH TO BENEFIT FROM THEM?
"THE SECURITY COMMITTEE FELT THAT THE PROJECT WAS TOO DANGEROUS. WE HAD TO HAVE SAFEGUARDS..."
"...I JUST HOPE WE DIDN'T UNDERESTIMATE THE SURVIVABILITY OF THE SUBJECTS..."
RESIST THE STATE
NADES
SKRRAKK!
RPG-7

BONK
AND YOU, PROFESSOR--OR SHOULD I CALL YOU ANDRE--?
DON'T EVEN TWITCH, AND KEEP THAT HOOK WHERE I CAN SEE IT!
ANDRE?
THAT NAME IS FROM A SUBJECT SCENARIO! HOW DO YOU--?
NAP-TIME, HINES--
HUH? THAT ROOM THEY'RE FIGHTING IN--!
--I KNOW THAT ROOM!!
YOU KNOW ABOUT THE WINDSOR SET?
WINDSOR? THAT WAS MY APARTMENT IN SAN FRANCISCO!
SILVER FOX!
WE LOST TRACK OF YOU TWENTY YEARS AGO!
YOU MESSED UP, BUB!
I CAN COME UP WITH MOVES YOU'VE NEVER SCANNED!
I GOT MOVES LIKE CARTERS GOT LITTLE PILLS!
YOUR RESISTANCE TO TERMINATION IS FUTILE, LOGAN!
SCHREKKKKKK!
I AM EQUIPPED WITH THE TRIG-GERS...

GAAAAAA!
...WHICH ARE ELECTRONIC PULSES THAT ACTIVATE NEURO-SYNTHETIC IMPLANTS IN YOUR CEREBRAL CORTEX!
IMPLANTS WHICH ACTIVATE A CATACLYSMIC MEMORY BACK-LASH!
ALL YOUR SUPPRESSED TRAUMA--
EVERY EXCRUCIATING MOMENT OF SEARING PAIN IN YOUR LIFE--
EVERY BULLET WOUND, SWORD CUT, LASER BLAST--
EVERY SECOND OF LONLINESS, HEART-BREAK AND SHAME--
--ALL VIVIDLY RECALLED WITH CHILLING CLARITY AND HORRIBLE DETAIL!
NOOOOOOOOooooooooOOOOOOOOOO
YOU CAN'T RUN AWAY FROM IT, LOGAN...
ASTROVILLE HIGH SENIOR PROM
...AND YOU CAN'T DEFEND YOURSELF WHILE YOUR OWN MEMORIES BETRAY YOU!

THAT GYM--
THOSE DECORATIONS--
THAT WAS MY SENIOR PROM!
SOMETHING HAPPENED THAT NIGHT, THAT I HAD FORGOTTEN...!!
MY TRIGGER PROGRAM CAN DO MUCH MORE THAN SIMPLY PARADE YOUR SUPPRESSED MEMORIES THROUGH YOUR CONSCIOUSNESS, LOGAN...
...IT CAN COMBINE THEM ALL IN A TEMPORAL NEXUS!
INSTEAD OF HAVING YOUR NIGHTMARES ONE AFTER THE OTHER--
--YOU CAN HAVE THEM ALL AT ONCE!
KILLRIPDIETEARRIPMURDERPUPILKILLFATHERMURDERSON!

--HUMAN!!

--LOGAN!!

YOU

CAN'T

KILL

ME

WITH

MEMORIES!!!!!!

YOU DON'T GET IT, DO YOU, GREASER?
THUNK
YOU JUST DON'T KNOW YOUR PLACE...!
WAP
...WHO DO YOU THINK YOU ARE --?
--BRINGIN' ONE OF THEM TO OUR PROM!
LOGAN...?
OH, LOGAN...
GET YER HANDS OFF ME!
BUT--
GO HOME--
--I DON'T WANNA SEE YOU ANY MORE.
NO!!!!!!
HE WOULDN'T HAVE DONE THAT!
THAT'S A LIE!! IT NEVER HAPPENED!
WHAT ABOUT THE CABIN????
THAT BLASTED CABIN IMPLANT!
IT LEAKS THROUGH THE SUPPRESSION PROGRAM IN EVERY SUBJECT!
THEY DON'T REMEMBER THEIR INTEGRAL WEAPONS SYSTEMS, BUT THAT IDIOTIC CABIN--
--GIVE ME THAT!!!!
BLAM! BLAM! BLAM! BLAM!

CYCLOPS, I TRACED THAT MYSTERIOUS LIST THROUGH ITS SUB-HEADINGS.
IT WAS STORED IN A FILE MARKED "TERMINATION PARAMETERS FOR PROJECT X"!
I'M AFRAID IT'S AN ELIMINATION PRIORITY!
BUT... WOLVIE'S FIRST ON THE LIST! WE'D BETTER GET DOWN THERE!

I AM DESIGNED AND PROGRAMMED FOR SURVIVABILITY, LOGAN!
I HAVE BACK-UP SYSTEMS FOR MY BACK-UP SYSTEMS ...!
...UNLIKE YOU!
I AM A TASK-SPECIFIC PROGRAM.
MY ONLY PURPOSE IS TO DESTROY SUBJECTS JUST LIKE YOU!
SCHREEEK!
NOBODY ELSE IS JUST LIKE ME!

SKREEEEEK!
...OR SHUT-DOWN OR WHATEVER A MACHINE DOES WHEN IT TAKES THE OBLIVION EXPRESS TO NOWHERE-VILLE!
TIME TO LAY DOWN AND DIE, ROBOT...!
SHEBA... WHAT KIND O' NAME IS THAT FOR A ROBOT?
SPAK! SSSHIVA! POP! THE TERRIBLE ASSSS-PECT OF RRRR! COSSS-MIC DISSSSOLUTION!
I AM RRRRR! A PRRROGRRAM, NOT POP! A ROBOT...
YOU CANNOT RRRRR! ESSSCAPE ME!
I AM POP! LEGION!
YOU'RE JUST A PILE O' SCRAP-METAL, BUB...

--AND YOU AIN'T EVEN SORTED FOR RE-CYCLING!
WOLVERINE--!
STAY BACK!
SCHREEEEK!
YOW! WATCH WHERE YOU SCATTER THAT JUNK--!
WOLVIE...?
DARLIN'--LEAVE ME BE...
SHUK!
SHUK!
AIIEEEEEEE
A WOMAN!
FROM DOWNSTAIRS!

WOLVIE...? THAT GUY LOOKS LIKE HE WAS RIPPED APART BY CLAWS!
HINES! YOU'RE HINES! I REMEMBER! WHAT HAPPENED? WHO DID THIS TO THE PROFESSOR?
I--I CAME TO... AND HE WAS DEAD!
RESET
DEFAULT
H--HIS HOOK WAS ACTIVATING THE RESET AND DEFAULT SWITCHES ON THE SHIVA OVERRIDE!
AND THEN I LOOKED UP AT THE SCREEN...

...THEY WERE ALL FILING OUT!
THEY WERE CHANTING A NAME-- LIKE A MANTRA--
--SABRE-TOOTH!
THE SHIVA PROGRAM JUST MOVED DOWN THE LIST TO THE NEXT NAME...

COULDN'T HAPPEN TO A NICER GUY...
...IT'S HIS PROBLEM, NOW.

LOGAN, WHAT ABOUT ALL THOSE OTHER CODE-NAMES ON THE LIST?
SOME OF THEM COULD BE MUTANTS WHO HAVE NO IDEA WHAT THEY REALLY ARE.
YEAH, AND WON'T KNOW THAT SOMETHING IS COMING AFTER THEM!
THEY MIGHT EVEN BE PEOPLE WE KNOW! HOW CAN YOU BE SO COLD? HOW CAN YOU JUST WALK AWAY? DON'T YOU CARE?!
I FEAR, MY X-MEN, THAT THE WOLVERINE THAT WAS REBORN TONIGHT MAY BE A FAR, FAR DIFFERENT MAN THAN THE ONE WE HAVE KNOWN.
HEAVEN HELP US ALL.
-fin.-

WOLVERINE #50 PINUP BY BILL SIENKIEWICZ

WOLVERINE #50 PINUP BY JIM LEE

MARVEL COMICS
WOLVERINE
SHIVA SCENARIO PART 1
© 1991 MARVEL ENT. GROUP, INC.
$1.75 US
$2.15 CAN
48
NOV
02254
APPROVED BY THE COMICS CODE AUTHORITY
BEGINNING: A QUEST INTO LOGAN'S PAST!
SILVESTRI + GREEN
THE SEQUEL TO WEAPON X
MEMORIES UNBOUND!

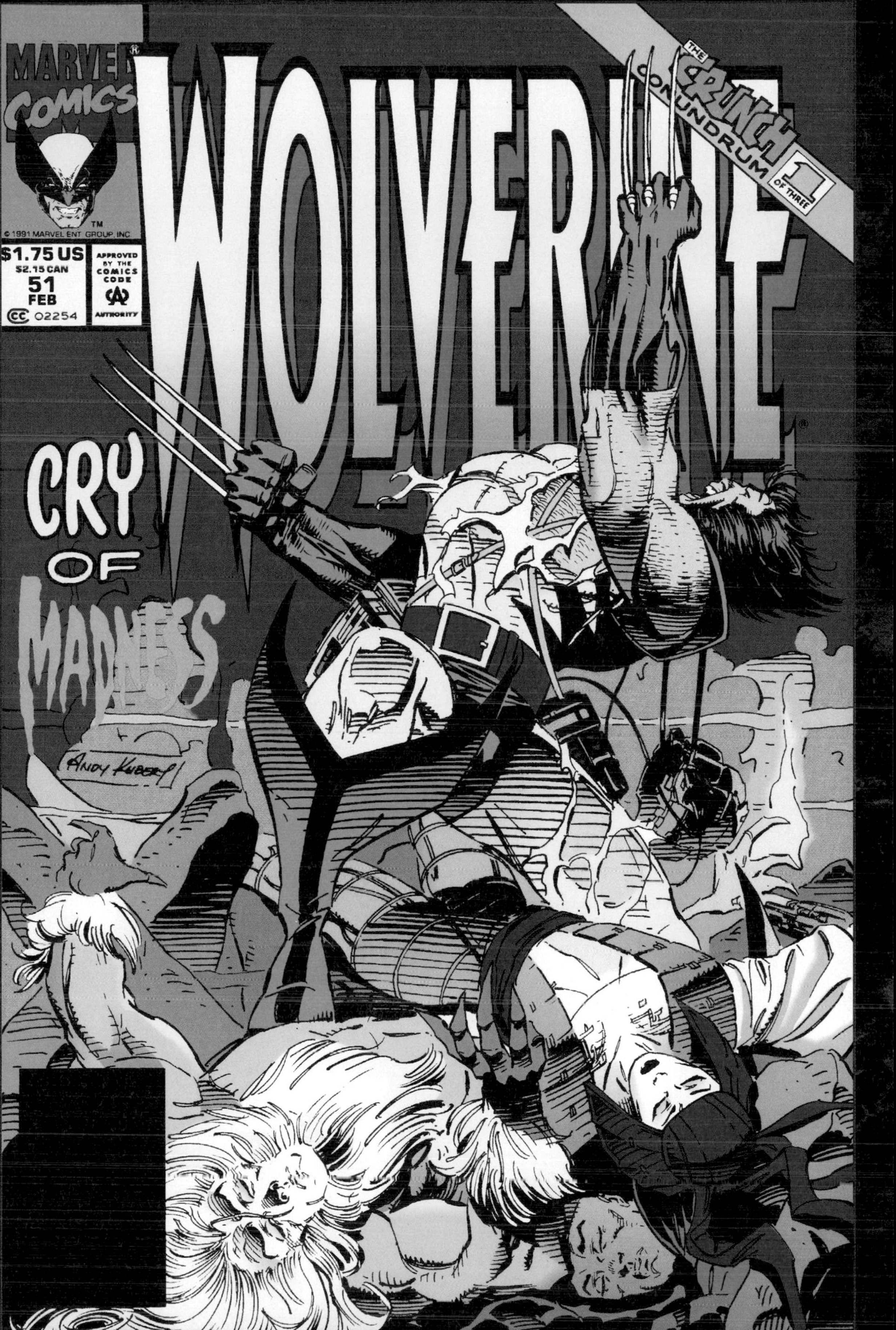

MARVEL COMICS
WOLVERINE
THE CRUNCH CONUNDRUM
1 OF THREE
© 1991 MARVEL ENT. GROUP, INC.
$1.75 US
$2.15 CAN
51
FEB
CC 02254
APPROVED BY THE COMICS CODE AUTHORITY
CRY OF MADNESS
Andy Kubert

STAN LEE PRESENTS:
HEARTBREAK MOTEL!
SCHRECK!
SKREEEEEEEEEEEEEEE
"WE'VE SET THE DANGER ROOM ATTACK SEQUENCE AT MAXIMUM THREAT FOR THE FULL SCALE SOLO COMBAT MODE..."
SCRIPT: LARRY HAMA
GUEST PENCILS: ANDY KUBERT
INKS: DAN GREEN
LETTERING: PAT BROSSEAU
COLORING: STEVE BUCCELLATO
EDITOR: BOB HARRAS
EDITOR IN CHIEF: TOM DeFALCO

...AND WE'RE NOT EVEN MONITORING VERY MUCH OF A HEARTBEAT AND RESPIRATION INCREASE IN WOLVERINE!
HE'S MAXING OUT THE SYSTEM WHILE COASTING IN NEUTRAL, BOSS. WE MIGHT AS WELL BE THROWING DAISIES AT HIM.
YOU'LL HAVE TO INCREASE HIS PERSONAL THREAT PROGRAM AT THE UPPER END OF THE SPECTRUM.
OH? AND WHAT ARE THE PARAMETERS, XAVIER?
THIS ISN'T NIGHT BASE-BALL--
YOU DON'T THINK WE'VE BEEN BATTING IN THE DARK ALL THIS TIME, FORGE?
CYCLOPS! STORM! THAT LAST COMBAT MODULE IS SNEAKING UP BEHIND WOLVIE--!
PATIENCE, JUBILEE. HE KNOWS IT IS THERE...
"...HE IS JUST PLAYING."

HO-HUM...
THAT THE BEST YOU CAN THROW AT ME?
THOUGHT THIS WAS THE DANGER ROOM.
OUGHTTA RENAME IT, OR YOU COULD BE SUED FOR FAKE ADVERTISIN'!
DO YOU FEEL LIKE "PUSHING THE ENVELOPE", LOGAN?
WOULD YOU LIKE US TO PROVIDE YOU WITH A REAL CHALLENGE?
I AIN'T GOIN' ANYWHERE.
HMMMM...
TOO MANY VARIABLES TO EXTRAPOLATE THE CONSEQUENCES ACCURATELY--
I DON'T NEED PSI-TALENT TO KNOW WHAT YOU'RE THINKING, PROFESSOR. WOLVERINE'S DIFFERENT, NOW--WILDER. THE REMOVAL OF THOSE MEMORY BLOCKS EFFECTED A PROFOUND CHANGE--*
EXACTLY.
WE DON'T KNOW HOW HE'S GOING TO REACT WHEN PUSHED TO THE EDGE--
--BUT ISN'T IT BETTER TO FIND OUT IN THE DANGER ROOM THAN IN THE REAL WORLD?
*WOLVERINE #49!
GET READY, WOLVERINE. I'M PUNCHING UP A NEW THREAT PROGRAM FOR YOU.
IF YOU WILL DON THE VIRTUAL REALITY VISUALIZER AND SENSORS, WE SHALL BEGIN...

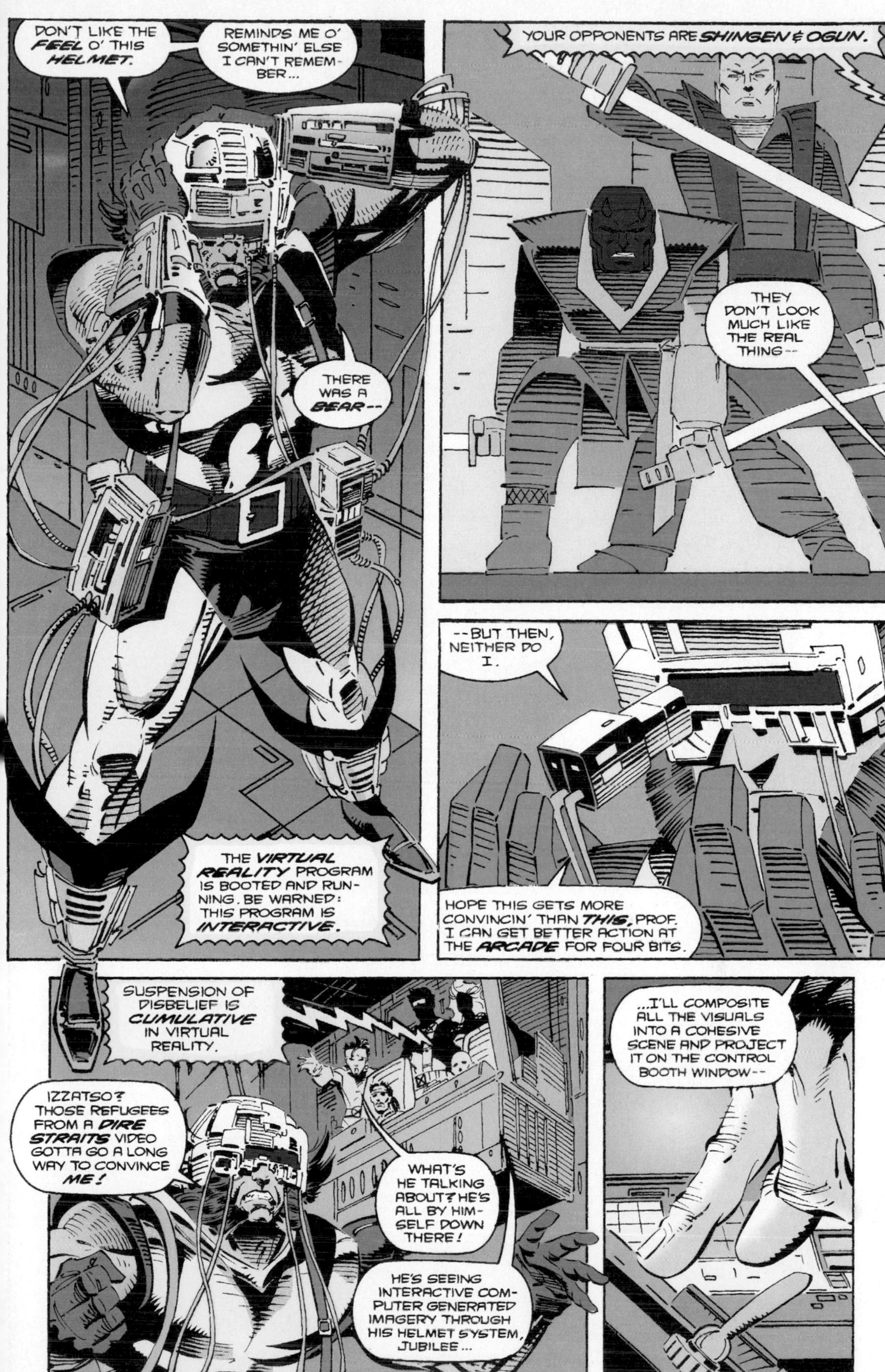
DON'T LIKE THE FEEL O' THIS HELMET.
REMINDS ME O' SOMETHIN' ELSE I CAN'T REMEMBER...
THERE WAS A BEAR--
THE VIRTUAL REALITY PROGRAM IS BOOTED AND RUNNING. BE WARNED: THIS PROGRAM IS INTERACTIVE.
YOUR OPPONENTS ARE SHINGEN & OGUN.
THEY DON'T LOOK MUCH LIKE THE REAL THING--
--BUT THEN, NEITHER DO I.
HOPE THIS GETS MORE CONVINCIN' THAN THIS, PROF. I CAN GET BETTER ACTION AT THE ARCADE FOR FOUR BITS.
SUSPENSION OF DISBELIEF IS CUMULATIVE IN VIRTUAL REALITY.
IZZATSO? THOSE REFUGEES FROM A DIRE STRAITS VIDEO GOTTA GO A LONG WAY TO CONVINCE ME!
WHAT'S HE TALKING ABOUT? HE'S ALL BY HIMSELF DOWN THERE!
HE'S SEEING INTERACTIVE COMPUTER GENERATED IMAGERY THROUGH HIS HELMET SYSTEM, JUBILEE...
...I'LL COMPOSITE ALL THE VISUALS INTO A COHESIVE SCENE AND PROJECT IT ON THE CONTROL BOOTH WINDOW--

--WITH A COMPUTER-GENERATED *WOLVERINE* SUPER-IMPOSED OVER THE REAL ONE.

WOW!

THAT WAS *SLICK!* CAN YOU CHANGE HIM INTO A *CAR?*

THIS IS AS FAST AS THESE GUYS CAN MOVE?

I'M SUPPOSED TO BE SCARED O' THESE CARTOONS--?

ZASSH!

SCHRIIKKK!

...AN' I'M GONNA SCATTER THEIR ELECTRONS!
HIGH-SPEED ATTACK SEQUENCE INITIATED--
SHUKKK!
SCHRIKK!
HOWD'JA LIKE THEM APPLES, HUH?
MESS WITH THE OL' ADAMANTIUM-LACED MUTANT--
--HE'LL PUT YA IN A WORLD O' HURT!
DON'T BOAST, GAIJIN!
THAT WAS WAZARE AT THE MOST--A HALF-POINT!
TO WIN A MATCH AGAINST SHINGEN & OGUN, YOU MUST SCORE IPPON--FULL POINT!
FULL POINT? I'LL GIVE YOU SIX FULL POINTS--
--RIGHT AT THE TIPS O' MY ADAMANTIUM STEEL CLAWS!

WHO'S HE TALKING TO? THOSE GUYS DIDN'T SAY ANY-THING!
HIS BRAIN IS AUGMENTING THE VISUAL INPUT-- SUPPLYING DIALOGUE--
AURAL HALLUCINATIONS? THIS HAS GONE TOO FAR--
"FLESHING OUT" IS A NORMAL REACTION TO THIS TYPE OF IMAGING. WE STILL HAVEN'T SEEN WHAT HE'LL DO IN AN OVER-THE-TOP STRESS SITUATION.
FORGE IS RIGHT...

...WE NEED TO KNOW THE FULL EXTENT OF THE CHANGE IN WOLVERINE.
I'M GOING TO DOUBLE THE THREAT LEVEL.

YOU BETTER KNOW WHAT YOU'RE DOING!

STAND BY, WOLVERINE...
...WE'RE THROWING LADY DEATH-STRIKE AND SABRE-TOOTH INTO THE MIX!

GONNA HAVE A REAL RIP AN' TEAR-FEST, HUH?
THE MORE THE MERRIER, AS FAR AS I'M CONCERNED.
COME ON!
LET'S BOOGIE--

--LET'S ROCK AND ROLL!
SCHRRRECK! ZESSH!
GNNGGH! NGRRRR!
"LOOK AT THESE BRAIN-WAVE PATTERNS!"
"EXTRAORDINARY."
"HE'S REGRESSED TO THE EMOTIONAL RESPONSE PATTERN OF A BESERKER KILLER APE...
"...BUT HE RETAINS HIGHLY SOPHISTICATED COMBAT SKILLS AND IS CAPABLE OF COMPLEX STRATEGIC DECISIONS WITHIN A COMPRESSED TIME FRAME!"
"THE EQUIVALENT OF AN OLYMPIC GYMNAST DOING A GOLD MEDAL ROUTINE WHILE SIMULTANEOUSLY BEATING FOUR CHESS COMPUTERS IN HIS HEAD!"

"ELAPSED TIME?"
"FROM INSERTION OF THE SABRETOOTH AND DEATH-STRIKE SIMULATIONS: 4.839 SECONDS TO EFFECTIVE NEU-TRALIZATION."

AWOOOOOOO
"WHY IS HE HOWL-ING? DO THE BRAIN WAVE MONITORS SHOW ANY REGRES-SIVE PATTERNS--?"
"NEGATIVE ACROSS THE BOARD. HE'S JUST...
"...LETTING OFF STEAM."
"THIS IS IN-TOLERABLE..."

...I WON'T BE PART OF THIS.
NEITHER WILL I.
HE RE-QUESTED THIS HIM-SELF--
HE DIDN'T ASK TO BE PUSHED TO THE EDGE OF HIS HUMANITY.

WHY IS WOLVIE DIFFERENT, PROFESSOR X...?
WAS IT WHAT HAPPENED UP IN CANADA?
THE MAN WE KNOW AS LOGAN HAS HAD HIS MEMORY TAMPERED WITH EXTENSIVELY...

...FOR ALL WE KNOW, THE PERSONALITY WE ARE SEEING NOW COULD BE HIS ORIGINAL, TRUE SELF.

LATER...
GOING *OUT*, HUH?
YEAH.
ON YOUR *SCOOT*, HUH?
YEAH.
COULD CATCH A *COLD* RIDING WITH YOUR HAIR WET--
NOT HARDLY.

CAN I--?
NO.
WHY *NOT*?
I AIN'T GOIN' TO NO PETTIN' ZOO.

GOING TO THAT HORRIBLE *AUGER INN* AGAIN?
WHAT DO YOU LIKE ABOUT THAT SLEAZY DIVE?
THE PRETZELS AIN'T SOGGY, THE POOL TABLE IS LEVEL, AND THE JUKEBOX IS CRANKED TO "TEN"...

LATER STILL...
AUGER INN
--EIGHT-BALL IN THE SIDE POCKET...
BUD

...AND THAT'S THE *GAME*.
WHO'S THE NEXT VICTIM?
I AM.
PONK!

STACK YER QUARTERS NEXT TO--
YES?
NEXT TO WHAT?

YOU DIDN'T GET DRESSED UP LIKE THAT TO SHOOT NO EIGHT-BALL WITH NO HOI-POLLOI.
YOU'RE ABSOLUTELY RIGHT.
THESE QUARTERS MIGHT BE BETTER SPENT ON *MUSIC*.

NAME YER POISON, DARLIN'.
ARE YOU GOING TO BUY ME A DRINK?
KIR.
BETTY
AIN'T GOT NO "KEER".

JUS' SHAKE SOME GRENADINE INTO A WHITE WINE FOR THE LADY.

THIS IS CERTAINLY AN ECLECTIC SELECTION.
WHAT DO PATSY CLINE, BUDDY HOLLY, OTIS REDDING AND STEVIE RAY VAUGHN HAVE IN COMMON?
IF ALL O' THEM HAD WAITED FOR THE BUS...
...THEY WOULD'VE GOT TO WHERE THEY WERE GOIN'.
IS THAT ZEN?
YEAH.
THAT WAS THEN.
AND THIS IS NOW.
Bud
NOT FOR MUCH LONGER.
DANCE WITH ME.
THIS SONG MAKES ME...
...LONELY.

HOW WOULD YOU LIKE TO COME SEE SOME REALLY AWFUL BLACK VELVET PAINTINGS OF BULL-FIGHTERS?
WHAT? NO ETCHINGS?
JUST BULL FIGHTERS...
...THAT'S ALL THEY HAVE ON MY MOTEL ROOM WALL.
AT THE X-MANSION...
THIS IS NO GOOD.
CAN'T TURN MY BRAIN OFF...
...AND IT'S STUCK ON A LOUSY CHANNEL.
NEED SOME AIR TO BLOW OUT THE COBWEBS...
...NEED SOME WIND IN MY FACE!

SHORTLY...
NO TRAFFIC AROUND HERE IN THE WEE HOURS.
I CAN REALLY GET SOME VELOCITY GOING.
WONDER IF THE AUGER INN IS STILL JUMPIN'?
WOLVIE'S BIKE ISN'T HERE!
I NEVER HEARD HIM COME BACK TO THE X-MANSION...
...WHERE COULD HE--?
--WHAT'S HIS BIKE DOING PARKED AT THIS PLACE?
Cloud 9 MOTEL
VACANCY
UGH.
TRIPLE 'UDE: RUDE, CRUDE AND LEWD!
MAYBE HE JUST WANTED TO BE ALONE SOMEWHERE!
RIGHT.
TIME TO SKATE ON HOME, GIRL, BECAUSE YOU'RE NO SNOOP AND LIKE HE SAID, WHAT'S IT TO YOU, AND--
--BUT WHAT IF HE'S IN TROUBLE?
VACANCY
WELL, HE COULD BE!

PLINK! PLINK!
PLUNK!
BZZNT!
KA-CHUNK!
WHO...
...IT'S *JEAN!!*
IT'S *JEAN GREY!!*
PZOK!

I TOLD YOU THAT WASN'T FUNNY.
...IRRESISTIBLE!
?
CHANGE BACK.
YOU LIKE THIS ONE, DO YOU?
NO.
BE YOURSELF.
I'VE HAD ENOUGH O' ILLUSION...
...MY WHOLE LIFE'S BEEN AN ILLUSION.
MORE'S THE PITY, EH, LOGAN...
THUNK!
WHAT WAS THAT NOISE?
MY SCOOT FELL OVER...
...I KNOW IT WAS SITTIN' SOLID ON ITS KICKSTAND.
SOME-BODY KICKED IT OVER!

FORGET ABOUT IT.
YOU KNOW, YOU WEREN'T COMPLAINING ABOUT THE ILLUSION A LITTLE WHILE AGO...
...REMEMBER THIS?
STOP IT.
WHAT'S GOT INTO YOU?
I'VE JUST DISCOVERED MYSELF.
I WANT TO HAVE FUN! I WANT TO LAUGH!
I FOOLED YOU, DIDN'T I? BACK AT THE BAR?

NAH. I KNEW YOU WERE REALLY MYSTIQUE AS SOON AS YOU WALKED IN.
CAN'T DISGUISE YOUR SCENT, DARLIN'.
OH? JUST PLAYING ALONG OUT OF SCIENTIFIC CURIOSITY? STRICTLY BUSINESS, MR. LOGAN? HA.

'CAUSE I SMELLED SOMETHIN' ELSE ON YOU.
FEAR.

ALWAYS HAD YOU PEGGED AS A COOL CUCUMBER. WHAT'S GOT YOU SWEATIN' BULLETS AND PULLIN' A STUNT LIKE THIS?
I...I DON'T EVEN WANT TO SAY HER NAME OUT LOUD...SHE'LL KNOW.

SHE'S GONE OFF THE DEEP END. SHE WAS NEVER REALLY SANE TO BEGIN WITH, BUT NOW--
WE GOT A "MYSTERY GUEST" OR WHAT? SHE BIGGER THAN A BREAD BOX? WHO'RE WE TALKIN' ABOUT HERE?

ELSEWHERE. DEEP BELOW NEW YORK CITY...
...IN THE PLACE CALLED MORLOCK ALLEY...
ALL OUR *BZZT* REPAIR WORK IS DONE, ELSIE-DEE.
IT'S *BZZT* TIME FOR US TO LEAVE THIS PLACE.
DON'T HURRY BACK. WE'RE CHANGING ALL THE LOCKS.
OH, MASQUE... COULDN'T YOU TWY TO BE NICE, PWEASE?
HRMPH! ERR ... ALBERT CERTAINLY DID A NICE JOB ON YOU. CAN'T HARDLY TELL YOU'VE BEEN REBUILT FROM THE NECK DOWN...
THANK YOU! ALBERT DUPWICATED THE EWECTWONICS THAT MR. PIERTHE DESIGNED FROM A BWUEPWINT IN MY MEMOWY!

IS THAT A FACT? MY, ISN'T THAT JUST PRECIOUS?
WELL, LET'S NOT HOLD YOU UP! GOTTA KEEP GOING ON YOUR MERRY ANDROID WAY!

...AND SOME OF MY SENSOR COMPONENTS EVEN CAME FWOM SPIWAL'S BODY SHOP--
--YOU'RE NOT WEALLY INTEWESTED, ARE YOU?

AWOOOOOOOO
IT'S THE LURKER! THE MONSTER FROM THE SEWERS!

HE'S TIRED OF EATING ALBINO 'GATORS AND NOW HE'S HUNGRY FOR MORLOCK!
ELSIE-DEE! TELL ALBERT TO TEAR ITS ARMS OFF!
OH, YOU JUST SHUSH, MASQUE!

HE'S WEALLY NOTHING MORE THAN A BIG PUPPY...
...AWEN'T YOU? AWWWW, NICE PUPPY! YOU DON'T BEWONG HERE, EITHER! YOU JUST COME WITH US!

...ALBERT BUILT THIS TUNNEL UNDER THE EAST WIVER SO HE COULD WORK ON WEPAIWING OUR STEALTH BOMBER!
HE CAN'T ƎBZTƐ UNDER-STAND YOU, ELSIE-DEE!
I KNOW THAT, SILLY! I JUST DIDN'T WANT HIM TO FEEL WEFT OUT--
ZZZZP! ZZZZP!
WHAT. WAS ƎBZTƐ THAT, ELSIE?
SOME OF MY SENSORS JUST WECAWIBWATED THEMSELVES ...
...AS IF THERE WAS A FWUX IN THE CONTINUUM!
IS THAT ƎBZTƐ BAD?
NO. JUST STWANGE.
OOOOOH, ALBERT!
YOU MADE IT WOOK WIKE YOU!
I'M GLAD ƎBZTƐ YOU LIKE IT, ELSIE-DEE!
SHE'S ƎBZTƐ TWICE AS STEAL-THY AS SHE WAS BEFORE AND NOW SHE HAS A STRANGE MAT-TER REACTOR JUST LIKE ƎBZTƐ THE ONE I INSTALLED IN YOU, ONLY BIGGER...

ARE YOU ALL =BZT= STRAPPED IN, ELSIE-DEE?
ALL SECURE, ALBERT!
AND SO IS PUPPY!
GRRRRRR!
WE'RE FREE, ELSIE...!
...FREE TO =BZT= SOAR LIKE EAGLES!
SHOOOOOM!
FREE!

AT THE MOTEL...
SINCE THE DISBANDING OF FREEDOM FORCE, AND DESTINY'S DEATH, I FELT YOU WERE THE ONLY ONE I COULD GO TO, AND I WASN'T EVEN SURE YOU WOULD HELP ME--
--THEY SAY YOU CHANGED.
DON'T CHANGE THE SUBJECT, DARLIN'.
DON'T SAY IT, WOLVERINE!
SHE HAS SENSOR PROBES THAT ARE GROWN IN METALLIC CRYSTAL BATHS WITHIN A ZERO-GRAVITY FIELD!
QUASI-SENTIENT SENSORS THAT CAN EDIT THEIR OWN DATA-FLOW!
YOU WERE ABOUT TO GIVE ME ANOTHER CLUE AS TO WHO IT IS THAT'S GOT YOU ALL IN A TIZZY...
...BUT DON'T EVEN BOTHER.
I GOT IT FIGURED--
"PARANOIA STRIKES DEEP", MYSTIQUE.
HER NAME'S A COMMON WORD. HOW CAN A MACHINE WEED IT OUT O' THE THOUSANDS O' TIMES IT'S SAID EVERY DAY?
YOU THINK OL' SPIRAL CAN--

--SPIRAL CAN!!
IT'S ALL IN THE CONTEXT, WOLVERINE!
CONTEXT AND NUANCE.
NEXT: OF MOJOS AND MANIACS!

MARVEL COMICS
WOLVERINE
THE CRUNCH CONUNDRUM
2 OF THREE
© 1992 MARVEL ENT. GROUP, INC.
$1.75 US
$2.15 CAN
52
MAR
APPROVED BY THE COMICS CODE AUTHORITY
02254
SILVESTRI & GREEN

CITADEL AT THE END OF TIME
THE CLOUD NINE MOTEL IN SALEM CENTER, WESTCHESTER COUNTY, NEW YORK...
THIS ROOM!
IT IS THE INTERSECTION OF FIVE DIFFERENT STRINGS IN THE TIME STREAM!
IT IS A CARDINAL LOCUS!
SPIRAL'S GONE COMPLETELY INSANE, WOLVERINE!
15
YOU CAN TELL THE DIFFERENCE, MYSTIQUE?
I ALWAYS FIGURED SHE HAD A FEW CHAIRS MISSIN' IN HER KITCHEN!
FOOLS!
A CARDINAL LOCUS CAN BE TRACED!
THERE ARE TOO MANY WEAK POINTS HERE--!
SCRIPT: LARRY HAMA
PENCILS: MARC SILVESTRI
INKS: DAN GREEN
COLORING: STEVE BUCCELLATO
LETTERING: PAT BROSSEAU
EDITOR: BOB HARRAS
EDITOR IN CHIEF: TOM DeFALCO
WACKO, RIGHT?

--TOO MANY NON-REFLECTIVE SURFACES!
ZASH!
RIGHT. ON HER BRAIN.
TOO LATE!
IT'S A TEMPORAL SEEKER BEAM!
SO BRIGHT--
--IT'S THE LIGHT OF A BILLION TOMORROWS!
I'M THINKIN': SHE'S A POETIC WACKO--
SZZZZZZZ!
--WHEN THE HAND COMES THROUGH.
THE REST IS NIGHTMARE ALLEY.
PICTURE AN ARC LAMP, WRAPPED IN ELECTRICAL TAPE AND LEAKIN' BEAMS O' TEN THOUSAND CANDLE-POWER.
SZZZZZZZ!
WHAT IS IT, SPIRAL?
PLASMA WRAITH!
WHATEVER IT IS, IT'S WARPIN' REALITY AROUND IT LIKE HEAT DISTORTION OFF A HOT PSYCHO'S HEAD...

...AN' IT'S REACHIN' OUT TO TOUCH ME WITH LESS THAN THE LIGHT O' HUMAN KINDNESS IN ITS EYES.
SCHRECK!
ZASH!
TIME TO DISPENSE SOME UNILATERAL DISARMAMENT, DARLIN'!
SHWOOOOOOP
IT'S AN ORDINARY PAINTING AGAIN...
ORDINARY? THAT MUST'VE SET THE CLOUD NINE BACK A GOOD DOUBLE-SAWBUCK!
I'M SHIELDING THE ROOM WITH A CLOAKING FIELD. WE NEED TIME TO ASSESS THIS SITUATION--
--THE WHOLE CONTINUUM IS RIVEN!
WASN'T A PERSON O' SUBSTANCE, HUH?
IT'S A SENTIENT ENERGY FIELD, WOLVERINE. LESS HEART THAN AN INSECT.

HOLD IT WIGHT HERE, ALBERT!
Cloud 9 MOTEL
VACANCY
BZT MAINTAINING HOVER, ELSIE-DEE!
...EVEN PUPPY WAS WEACTING!
BUT NOW, NOT A GWIMMER!
I WAS CATCHING THE STWANGEST VIBES FWOM THIS PWACE!
ALL MY METAWWIC CWYSTAL, SPIWAL-BUILT SENSORS WERE GOING CWAZY...
OH WELL--
WET'S GO, ALBERT--!
--NORTH TO CANADA! FULL STEALTH MODE!
Cloud 9 MOTEL
VACANCY
HUH?
--COULD'VE SWORN SOMETHING BIG JUST FLEW OVERHEAD!

SPIRALS TO THE N^TH POWER!
I HAVE ENTERED/ AM ENTERING/ WILL BE ENTERING THE TIME STREAM AT A NUMBER OF LOCI THAT IS AN INFINITE GEOMETRIC SERIES CONVERGING TO A/(1-R)!
SHE'S RAVING --
YOU'RE TALKIN' CRAZY, SPIRAL--
OF COURSE
I'M
NOT
SANE!
SANITY IS SIMPLY THE DENIAL OF CHAOS!
YOU CAN'T HAVE MULTIPLE TEMPORAL EXISTENCES IN A SANE UNIVERSE!
CHUK!
THERE!
IN THE CATHODE BEAM POLARIZED BY MY SWORD-- THE SHADES OF THE ONCE AND FUTURE SPIRAL--
--ALL DANCING TOWARDS THE TEMPORAL CONVERGENCE ...
...THE CRUNCH!
BZZZZZZ

HAVIN' A CONVENTION O' YOURSELF, ARE YA?
I AM NOT THE ONLY ONE.
THERE IS A TRAFFIC JAM IN THE TIME STREAM.
EVERY TIME SHIFTER, TRANS-DIMENSIONAL TRIPPER AND SPACE-TIME JUGGLER IN THE CONTINUUM IS HURTLING TOWARDS THE CRUNCH IN MULTIPLE EXISTENCES...
...SOME ARE OLD ACQUAINTANCES OF YOURS.
WHAT'S THIS CRUNCH?
SOUNDS CRISPY.
THE UNIVERSE BEGAN WITH THE BIG BANG.
IT ENDS WITH THE CRUNCH.

BZZZZAP!
SPIRAL!
WHAT ARE YOU --?

THAT'S NOT ME!!!
Cloud 9 MOTEL
VACANCY
VRRRUM!

DRAT.
MY SKATE-LACE HAS JOINED THE RANKS OF THE UNTIED.

LACES ARE SO RETRO-TECH.
DON'T THEY KNOW THAT THE FUTURE BELONGS TO VELCRO--?
ZZZZAPP!
WEIRD NOISE--
--500 POUND BEE? KLINGON DEATH RAY? NONE OF THE ABOVE?

--SOMETHING IN THE FUTURE SENT IT BACK ALONG THE SEEKER BEAM AND HOMED IN ON MY SWORD CIRCUITS!
THOOP!
IT'S AN UN-CERTAINTY NULLIFIER--!
WHATEVER YOU SAY, DARLIN'.
IT'S ALL PSYCHO-BABBLE, RIGHT?
PSYCHO-BABBLE DOESN'T USUALLY BURN NEAT HOLES THROUGH THE LEVELORS.
AS LONG AS WE ARE IN THE PAST IN RELATION TO WHATEVER SENT THAT UNCERTAIN-TY NULLIFIER, WE ARE VULNERABLE!!
YOU'RE NOT TAKING US INTO THE FUTURE??
"FUTURE" HAS NO MEANING WHERE WE ARE GOING!
IT IS A PLACE WHERE TIME FOLDS IN ON ITSELF!
SOUNDS LIKE A BAR I KNOW IN POUGH-KEEPSIE...

NOW, WHAT?
NOW WE HAVE TORNADOS IN WEST-CHESTER!
VACAN
OH, THIS IS JUST THE LIMIT!
GOTTA BE PART OF THAT GLOBAL WARMING MESS--ALL THOSE FLUORO-CARBONS EATING HOLES IN THE OZONE AND--

VACANCY
--WHOA!!
THIS WHIRLWIND UNDERTOW IS SUCKING ME RIGHT IN--!

--AND I HAVE A FEELING THAT WHATEVER GETS PULLED IN THERE DOESN'T GET A ROUSING MUNCHKIN WELCOME FROM THE LOLLIPOP GUILD!
WOLVIE! ARE YOU IN THERE?

WOLV--
--HUH?

BONK!
WHO TURNED OFF THE BREEZE?

WOW.
TALK ABOUT *MINIMAL FURNISH-INGS...*
...*WAITAMINUTE...*
WOLVIE'S *MOTOR-CYCLE* GOT SUCKED IN HERE!
WHERE DID *IT* GO TO?
NOT *WHERE*, LITTLE X-MAN, BUT *WHEN!*
WHO SAID THAT?

SURPRISE!
SURPRISE!
SURPRISE!
MOJO!!

ELSEWHEN...
TIME VORTEX...
I'VE BEEN THROUGH ONE O' THESE BEFORE.
LAST TIME, I WENT BACK TO GUERNICA...
THIS TIME-- THAT'S A LAUGH... IT'S ALREADY NEXT TIME!

AT LEAST THERE AIN'T NO SENSE O' DREAD, GOIN' TOWARDS THE FUTURE IN A TIME VORTEX.
WE'RE OVERTAKIN' THE NEXT MOMENT TOO FAST TO FEAR IT.

WHAT'S THAT LIGHT, SPIRAL?
THAT'S NOT LIGHT!
THAT'S A HOLE IN TIME!
A DIRECT WARP TO THE CRUNCH!
WHAT HAPPENS TO PEOPLE WHEN THEY GO THROUGH SOMETHIN' LIKE THAT?

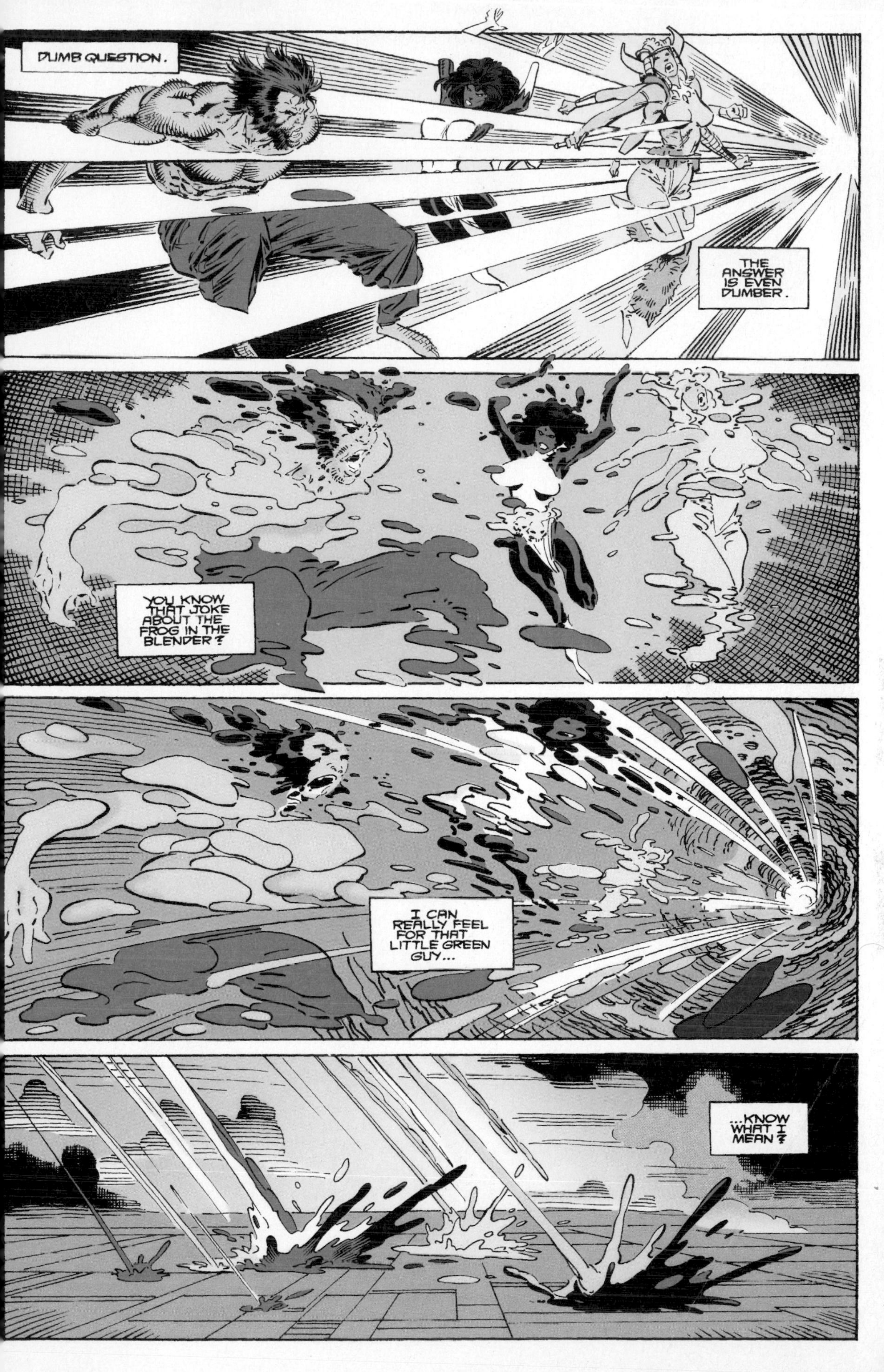
DUMB QUESTION.
THE ANSWER IS EVEN DUMBER.
YOU KNOW THAT JOKE ABOUT THE FROG IN THE BLENDER?
I CAN REALLY FEEL FOR THAT LITTLE GREEN GUY...
...KNOW WHAT I MEAN?

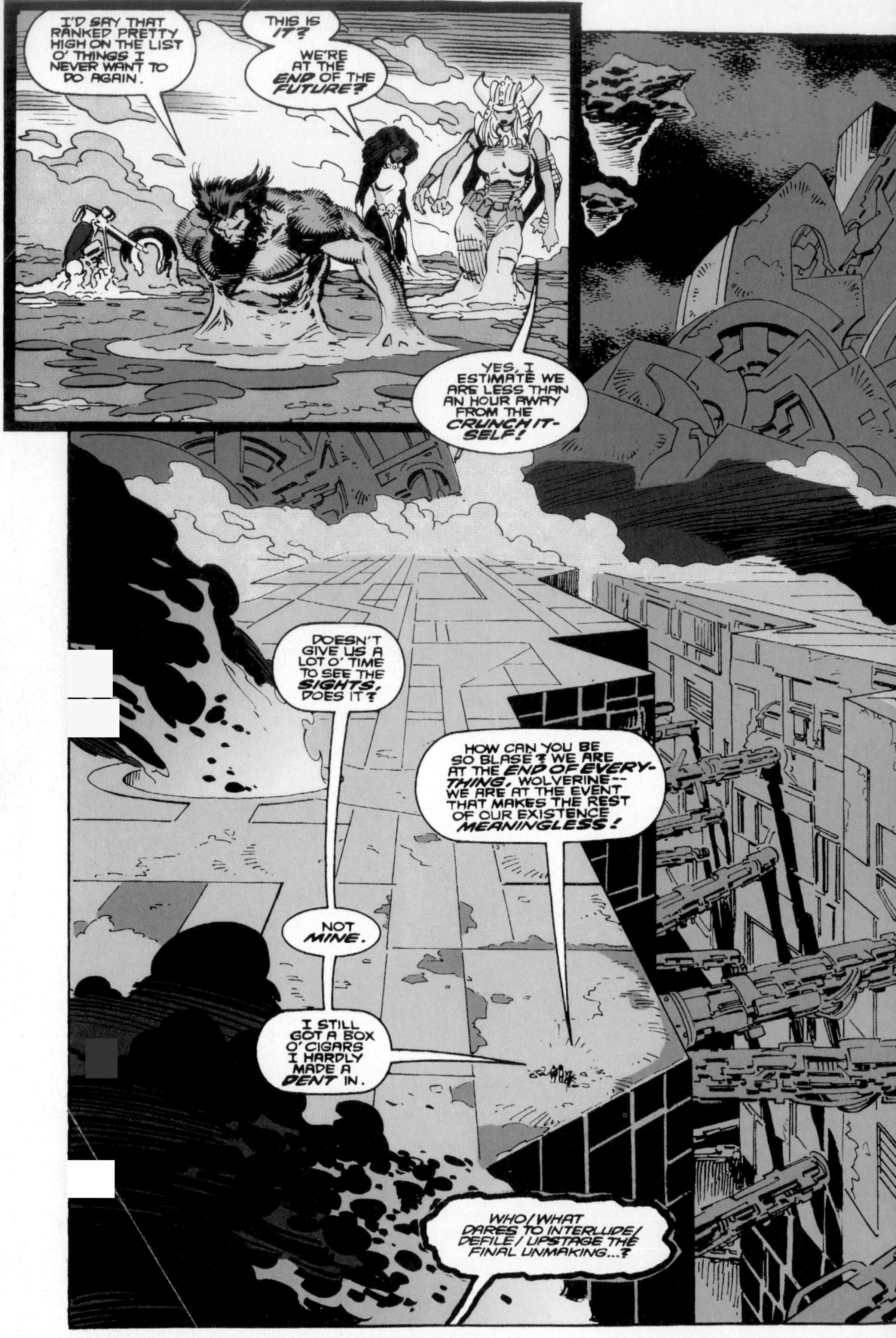
I'D SAY THAT RANKED PRETTY HIGH ON THE LIST O' THINGS I NEVER WANT TO DO AGAIN.
THIS IS IT?
WE'RE AT THE END OF THE FUTURE?
YES, I ESTIMATE WE ARE LESS THAN AN HOUR AWAY FROM THE CRUNCH IT-SELF!
DOESN'T GIVE US A LOT O' TIME TO SEE THE SIGHTS, DOES IT?
HOW CAN YOU BE SO BLASÉ? WE ARE AT THE END OF EVERY-THING, WOLVERINE-- WE ARE AT THE EVENT THAT MAKES THE REST OF OUR EXISTENCE MEANINGLESS!
NOT MINE.
I STILL GOT A BOX O' CIGARS I HARDLY MADE A DENT IN.
WHO/WHAT DARES TO INTERLUDE/ DEFILE/ UPSTAGE THE FINAL UNMAKING...?

BILATERALLY SYMMETRICAL SOFT/SHORT-LIVED FATTY TISSUE BEINGS WITH VERTEBRAE--
--PASTLINGS!!
ANOTHER PLASMA WRAITH!
PASTLINGS NOT DIRECTING/ INVOLVED/CAST IN THE GREAT WORK!!
I WILL KILL/ DEVOLVE/ TEMPORALLY DISLOCATE YOU FOREVER!

SOME THREAT!
FOREVER'S JUST ABOUT UP!
SENTIENT MEAT/ MOBILE PROTEIN/ PROTOPLASM WITH COMPLEX PAIN RE-CEPTORS!
FOREVER RUNS BOTH WAYS, WOLVERINE!
SHE CAN PUT YOU OUT OF SYNCH WITH TIME. PHASE YOU BACK-WARDS ALWAYS JUST A NANO-SECOND BEFORE NOW!
IMAGINE YOUR CONSCIOUS-NESS STABILIZED, AWARE, TRAPPED IN NULL-TIME AS THE UNIVERSE TICKS BACK TO THE BEGINNING --?
SCHRECK!
YOU TREAD ON THE CUSP OF FEAR/PAIN/ DEATH!
THAT MEAN YOU WANT FIRST DIBS ON HER, SPIRAL?
HOWSABOUT SOME SLICE/DICE AND --
TCHK!
--UNGHHHH!
HOTTER'N A BLAST FURNACE!
HURT, MEAT THING? HURT FOR NEVER-MORE!
SZZZZZ!

WHAT GIVES, SPIRAL? THAT OTHER WRAITH WE CHOPPED UP BACK AT THE MOTEL DIDN'T HAVE ITS THERMOSTAT TURNED UP LIKE THIS ONE!
THAT WAS A MERE SHADE OF THE REAL THING--
HERE AND NOW IN THEIR OWN PLACE AND TIME, THEIR POWER IS CONCENTRATED
LEAVE THOSE DISGUSTING SPINED THINGS ALONE!
THE PRODUCER/ DIRECTOR/ WRITER--
--THE AUTEUR!!
MOJO BY ANY OTHER NAME WOULD SMELL AS SWEET!
NOW! WHILE SHE'S DISTRACTED AND CON-FUSED--!
--STRIKE!
SCHRACK!
SCHRECK!!

SLICK MOVE, MYSTIQUE. HOW'D YOU KNOW MOJO WAS BEHIND THIS SCAM?
THE WRAITH WAS BABBLING MOVIE-JARGON...
WHO ELSE NAVIGATES TIME, SPACE AND WANTS TO MAKE MOVIES?
MOJO'S REALLY DONE IT THIS TIME...

...HE'S LET LOOSE A JUGGERNAUT OF CIRCUMSTANCES THAT THREATENS ALL EXIS-TENCE--
--AND THE ONLY WAY TO STOP IT IS TO GET INSIDE THE CITADEL AT THE END OF TIME!

SO WHERE IS THIS CITADEL, DARLIN'?

WE'RE STANDING ON IT.

MEANWHEN, IN WESTCHESTER...
--LOOK... I'M OUT OF HERE!
GOT THINGS TO DO. PLACES TO BE, PEOPLE TO SEE--
DON'T BE SUCH A GLOOM! THE PARTY IS JUST BE-GINNING!
WE'RE ALL GOING TO HAVE SUCH MURDEROUS FUN--!
NO WAY! I'M HISTORY--!
SLAM!
YOU'RE STAYING!
I INSIST!
YOU'RE NOT GOING ANYWHERE UNTIL YOU TELL ME WHERE OR WHEN MY EX-SLAVE AND MAGICKAL PROTEGE HAS GONE OFF TO!
WHERE IS THAT MULTI-APPENDAGED BAROQUE VIXEN?
SHE WAS HERE! THE AIR IS ALIVE WITH HER ION-TRAIL--
PAF!
GIVE IT A BREAK--!
--I HOPE I FRIED YOUR RETINAS TO A CRISPY WELL-DONE, YOU METAL-DREADED JELLO-BUCKET--
I'LL HAVE YOUR DISKS COMPACTED, YOU PERNICIOUS SLANDERER--!
--SIC HER, MY PET!
YOU'RE SICCING THAT ON ME?
SHHHHHHH!

WHAT'S SHE GOING TO DO... DEAFEN ME WITH CHAIN-RATTLING?

DO HER, ABCISSA!

I WANT HER WRAPPED UP TO TAKE BACK WITH US!

AS YOU COMMAND.

A TOSS OF THE HEAD; THE FUN HAS BEGUN!

A LOOP...

UH-OH!

AND A TWIST...

...AND THE CIRCLE IS DONE!

NOW BEGINS THE DANCE!

PLAY, YOU SPACE/TIME GYPSIES!

GIVE US A LIVELY GAVOTTE--

IN CANADA...
--STWANGE. THIS WHOLE ABANDONED FACIWITY BEWOW US DOESN'T APPEAR ON ANY OF THE SURVEY MAPS!
KEEP OUT
IMPOSSIBLE TO ≡BZT≡ ACCESS FILE DATA ON THIS LOCATION, ELSIE-DEE--IT'S ALL ≡BZT≡ LOCKED OUT WITH SECURITY SHIELDS.
STWANGER AND STWANGER! WHY WOULD A GOVERNMENT AGENCY BUILD A COVERT SITE ADJACENT TO AN ANCIENT BWACKFOOT BUWIAL GWOUND?
NOTHING HERE IS ≡BZT≡ CONSISTENT WITH KNOWN FUNERARY PRACTICES IS ≡BZT≡ SIKSIKA, KINAH AND PIKUNI INDIGENOUS TRIBAL GROUPS AS ≡BZT≡ AVAILABLE IN ACCESSABLE DATA BANKS.
WHY IS OUR ≡BZT≡ FURRY FRIEND SO INTERESTED IN THIS ≡BZT≡ PATCH OF WILDERNESS? WHY DID HE ≡BZT≡ LEAD US HERE?
I DON'T KNOW, ALBERT! BUT PUPPY CERTAINWY SEEMS TO BE TEWWIBWY EXCITED TO BE HERE!
HE'S POINTING AT THAT MOUND AND CAWWYING ON SO!
LET'S ≡BZT≡ TAKE A LOOK. I'LL ≡BZT≡ PARK US ON HOVER...
BEEN UPGWADING THE CWUISE MISSILES, ALBERT? THIS NUKE WOOKS ALBERT-IZED!
NOT A ≡BZT≡ NUKE ANY LONGER...
...IT'S A ≡BZT≡ ANTI-MATTER IMPLOSION INITIATOR.

HE WANTS ME TO ≡BZT≡ HELP HIM DIG INTO THIS ≡BZT≡ MOUND!
YOU BOYS GO WIGHT AHEAD AND PWAY IN THE DIRT!
I'M GOING TO KEEP MY PWETTY NEW DWESS CWEAN!
WOOK, ALBERT!
THERE'S WEAL BUTTER-FWIES HERE!
YOU HAD BETTER ≡BZT≡ COME TAKE A LOOK AT THIS, ELSIE-DEE!
WE JUST FOUND A ≡BZT≡ SKELETON!
SO WHAT, ALBERT? THIS PWACE IS FULL OF SKEWETONS!
NOT LIKE ≡BZT≡ THIS ONE, ELSIE...
...THIS ≡BZT≡ ONE HAS ≡BZT≡ ADAMANTIUM CLAWS!
NEXT MONTH:
MAYHEM AT TIME'S END!

Marvel Comics ILLUSTRATION QUALITY PAPER FOR REGULAR COMIC PAGES
Book WOLVERINE Issue # 52 pg # 2
2
—TOO MANY NON-REFLECTIVE SURFACES!
ZASH!
RIGHT. ON HER BRAIN.
TOO LATE!
IT'S A TEMPORAL SEEKER BEAM!
SO BRIGHT--
--IT'S THE LIGHT OF A BILLION TOMORROWS!
I'M THINKIN': SHE'S A POETIC WACKO--
SZZZZZZZ!
--WHEN THE HAND COMES THROUGH.
THE REST IS NIGHTMARE ALLEY.
PICTURE AN ARC LAMP, WRAPPED IN ELECTRICAL TAPE AND LEAKIN' BEAMS O' TEN THOUSAND CANDLE-POWER.
SZZZZZZZ!
WHAT IS IT, SPIRAL?
PLASMA WRAITH!
WHATEVER IT IS, IT'S WARPIN' REALITY AROUND IT LIKE HEAT DISTORTION OFF A HOT PSYCHO'S HEAD...

MARVEL COMICS
WOLVERINE
© 1992 MARVEL ENT. GROUP, INC.
$1.75 US
$2.15 CAN
53
APR
02254
APPROVED BY THE COMICS CODE AUTHORITY
THE CRUNCH CONUNDRUM
3 OF THREE
TIME, SPACE, AND MOJO TOO!!
SILVESTRI × GREEN

THE UNIVERSE BEGAN WITH THE BIG BANG, IT ENDS WITH THE CRUNCH...
...SO THIS WHOLE PLANETOID IS SOMETHIN' CALLED THE CITADEL AT THE END OF TIME?
THIS IS THE LAST STOP ON THE COSMIC EXPRESS AND MOJO IS HERE MESSIN' WITH THE TRACK SWITCHES?
THAT'S ABOUT THE SIZE OF IT, WOLVERINE.
AN' YOU FIGGER OL' MOJO HIMSELF IS DOWN INSIDE THE CITADEL?
HE DOWN THERE GETTIN' HIS JOLLIES, SPIRAL?
HE LIKES TO BE WHERE THE ACTION IS. HE LIKES TO WATCH.
WHAT SAY WE HEAD DOWN-STAIRS AND BARK HIS SHINS?
FEEL THE NEED TO GET SUITED UP FOR THIS?
WOULDN'T WANT IT SAID THAT THE UNIVERSE ENDED, AND I WAS UNDER-DRESSED, MYSTIQUE DARLIN'.
CLIMB ON THE SCOOT, GIRLS. TIME TO RATTLE MOJO'S CAGE.

HOW DO YOU INTEND RIDING INTO THE CITADEL?
THERE AREN'T ANY RAMPS-- JUST THESE ENORMOUS STEEP-SIDED CRATERS...
EVER BEEN TO AN OLD-TIME STATE FAIR?
EVER SEE A BARREL RIDER?
NO...
I HOPE YOU KNOW WHAT YOU'RE DOING!
THEN HANG ON, DARLIN'-- YOU'RE IN FOR A TREAT!
IF I LET THAT STOP ME, I'D NEVER DO ANY-THIN'!
SCRIPT--LARRY HAMA
PENCILS--MARC SILVESTRI
INKS--DAN GREEN WITH AN ASSIST FROM BARTA & JANSON
COLORING--ROSAS/TINSLEY/JAVINS
LETTERING--PAT BROSSEAU
EDITOR--BOB HARRAS
EDITOR IN CHIEF--TOM DeFALCO

LIGHTEN UP, MYSTIQUE!
WE'VE GOT CENTRIFUGAL FORCE ON OUR SIDE...!
THE CHIMERICAL MYSTERY TOUR!

...AS LONG AS WE MAINTAIN ENOUGH VELOCITY WE'RE PERFECTLY--
HMMMM...
THIS IS NOT A SOLID SURFACE WE'RE RIDING ON!

WHAT IS IT????
IT'S A JAM!
A MASTER-WORK CRAFTED BY A MILLION AL-TERNATE EXISTENCES OF UMPTEEN SPACE-TIME JUGGLERS!
NOW WHAT???
JUST RODE INTO THE SHADOW O' THE CRATER, DARLIN'...
CLICK!
...I'LL JUST SNAP ON THE HEADLAMP--

THE RIM!!!!!
WE'RE GOING TO GO OVER THE RIM OF THE VORTEX!
THAT WAS THE GREAT MOTHER OF ALL TIME VORTEXES!

THAT WAS A TIME VORTEX?
WHY WEREN'T WE SWEPT INTO ANOTHER CONTINUUM?
KNOW ANYTHING ABOUT QUANTUM CHROMODYNAMICS? IT'S REALLY QUITE SIMPLE--
SHUT UP, SPIRAL!
I WANT TO BE ABLE TO HEAR MYSELF SCREAM BEFORE WE GO SPLAT!

DO THAT!
JUST MAKE SURE YOU'RE FACING A HOLOVISION SENSOR!
MOJO!
GETTING ALL THIS ON DIGITAL LASER ARE YOU?
WHERE IS THAT FAT GEEK?
IS THIS ALL JUST ANOTHER ONE OF HIS STUPID MOVIES?
GEEK????
YOU'VE GOT SOME NERVE, YOU DISGUSTING SPINED THING, YOU!!!
HE'S JUST A PROJECTION ON A GIANT HIGH DEFINITION TV SCREEN!
ULTRA GAS-PLASMA, TO BE PRECISE...
...NOW REALLLY-- I MUST INSIST ON QUIET ON THE SET!
BONK!

HOW DO YOU EXPECT ME TO GET A DECENT PERFORM-ANCE OUT OF MY INGENUE WHEN YOU SUPERNUMERARIES ARE MAKING SUCH A RACKET!
WOLVIEEEEEEE!
JUBILEE!
LET HER GO, YA BIG-TOOTHED FISH-EYED LARD-BUCKET!
SCHRECK!
PASTLINGS/ PROTO-PLASMIC PROTEINS/ SET-CRASHERS!
PLASMA WRAITHS!
DOES MOJO/AUTEUR DESIRE THEIR NULLIFICATION WITH FEAR/PAIN/ PROTRACTED SUFFERING?
OH, YES!
ESPECIALLY THE PROTRACTED SUFFERING!

CANADA.
THE PRESENT.
WHAT KIND OF TESTS ARE YOU WUNNING ON THE SKEWETON NOW, ALBERT?
I ≡BZT≡ SCANNED THE SKULL CONTOURS AND ≡BZT≡ BUILT A DIGITILIZED COMPUTER MODEL.
NOW, I'M ≡BZT≡ RUNNING THE FACIAL RECONSTRUCTION PROGRAM-- IT ≡BZT≡ FLESHES OUT THE BONE AND EXTRAPOLATES THE FEATURES, ELSIE-DEE.
≡BZT≡ SPECTROSCOPIC ANALYSIS CONFIRMS ≡BZT≡ ADAMANTIUM CLAWS. ALSO, ≡BZT≡ ADAMANTIUM BONDED TO INTERNAL STRUCTURE OF ≡BZT≡ BONES...
DID YOU CAWBON-DATE THE SKEWETON?
TOO ≡BZT≡ RECENT...
...HAD TO ≡BZT≡ DATE BY COMPARATIVE RATE OF ≡BZT≡ SOLUBLE MINERAL LEACHING--
--THE ≡BZT≡ RECONSTRUCTION IS COMPLETE!
GRRRRR!
OH, ALBERT! THE RESEMBWANCE IS CWEEPY...!
...BUT IT CAN'T WEALLY BE WOGAN! THIS SKEWETON WOOKS TOO OLD!
≡BZT≡ OVER TWO HUNDRED YEARS OLD, TO BE ≡BZT≡ EXACT, ELSIE!

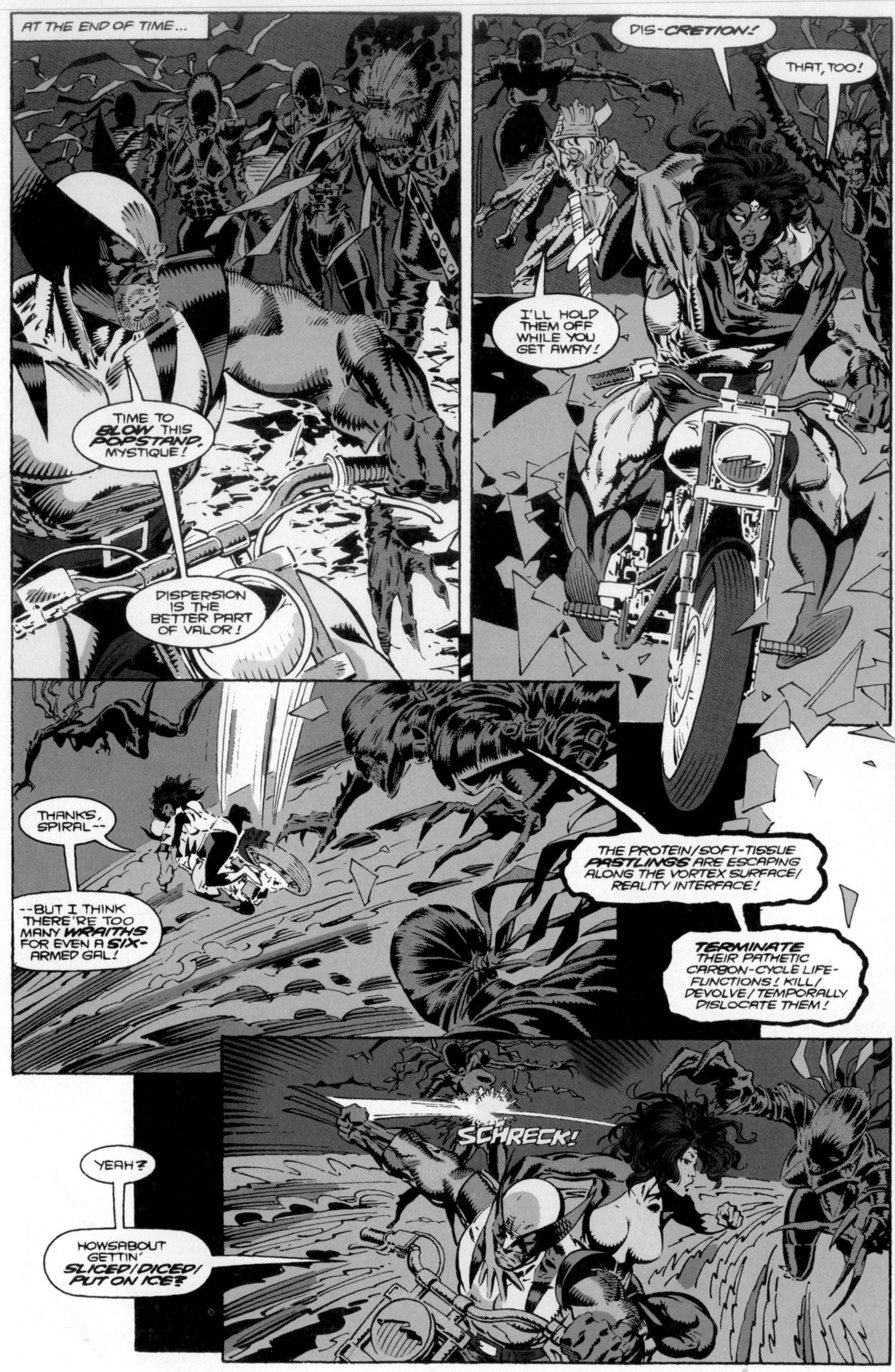
AT THE END OF TIME...
TIME TO BLOW THIS POPSTAND, MYSTIQUE!
DISPERSION IS THE BETTER PART OF VALOR!
DIS-CRETION!
THAT, TOO!
I'LL HOLD THEM OFF WHILE YOU GET AWAY!
THANKS, SPIRAL--
--BUT I THINK THERE'RE TOO MANY WRAITHS FOR EVEN A SIX-ARMED GAL!
THE PROTEIN/SOFT-TISSUE PASTLINGS ARE ESCAPING ALONG THE VORTEX SURFACE/ REALITY INTERFACE!
TERMINATE THEIR PATHETIC CARBON-CYCLE LIFE-FUNCTIONS! KILL/ DEVOLVE/ TEMPORALLY DISLOCATE THEM!
SCHRECK!
YEAH?
HOWSABOUT GETTIN' SLICED/DICED/ PUT ON ICE?

SKREEEEE!
THESE UNDERLINGS ARE JUST WASTING OUR TIME...
...WE HAVE TO GET TO THE ROOT OF THIS PROBLEM!

WE HAVE TO STOP MOJO!
ALL RIGHT BY ME, DARLIN'. I'M ALWAYS DOWN FOR SOME UNIVERSE-SAVIN'--
YOU DON'T UNDERSTAND!
WHAT MOJO IS DOING IS PRE-VENTING THE CRUNCH! THE VORTEX HE CRE-ATED IS STALLING THE BIG IMPLOSION OF EVERY-THING!
BECAUSE HE WANTS MORE FOOTAGE FOR HIS HOLO-VISION MOVIES, RIGHT?

RIGHT!
BUT HE DIDN'T THINK IT ALL THE WAY THROUGH! HE NEVER DOES! IF THE CRUNCH DOESN'T HAPPEN, THE BIG BANG COULDN'T HAVE HAPPENED! WITHOUT AN END THERE IS NO BE-GINNING!
AIN'T THIS SOMETHIN'?
IN ORDER TO SAVE THE UNIVERSE, WE HAVE TO DESTROY IT!

DO YOU HEAR THEM, JUBILEE?
THEY THINK THAT I DON'T KNOW WHAT I'M DOING!!
MAYBE I WANT EVERYTHING TO END!
MAYBE I'VE GOT IT FIGURED SO THAT EVERYTHING BUT ME-- AND A FEW SELECTED ENTITIES BLINK OFF INTO NOTHINGNESS!
MAYBE MY NEW SPACE/TIME SKATER, ABCISSA CAN CUT A FEW COSMIC FIGURE-EIGHTS THAT NO ONE EVEN DREAMED OF!
AND MAYBE YOU'RE SERIOUSLY MISSING A SET OF CHAIRS FROM YOUR DINETTE SET!
YOU CAN SEE WHO IS HOLDING THE WINNING HAND HERE! I'M AFRAID YOUR LITTLE HIRSUTE FRIEND IS DOOMED, AS IS THE ENTIRE UNIVERSE...
...UNLESS, OF COURSE, YOU AND I CAN COME TO AN AGREEMENT!
PROFESSOR XAVIER WARNED ME ABOUT CREEPS LIKE YOU!
I'M SURE HE DID. WANT TO HEAR MY DEAL?
HOW YUCKED-OUT IS IT?
NOT TOO UNPLEASANT AT ALL...
...YOU SIMPLY CONSENT TO BEING MY SLAVE!

LOOK!
THE SWIRLING IMAGES WITHIN THE VORTEX ARE COALESCING!
ONE OF THE TIME-SHIFTERS OR DIMENSIONAL JUGGLERS TRAPPED WITHIN THE VORTEX BY MOJO IS EXERTING ENOUGH WILL TO MAKE HIMSELF KNOWN TO US!
I KNOW THAT LUG...

...THAT'S GATEWAY!
WHAT'S HE TRYIN' TO TELL US?
LOOK AT HIS BULL-ROARER...!

...THAT'S NO ABORIGINE-BUILT WHIRLIGIG!
I KNOW WHAT THAT IS, DARLIN'...
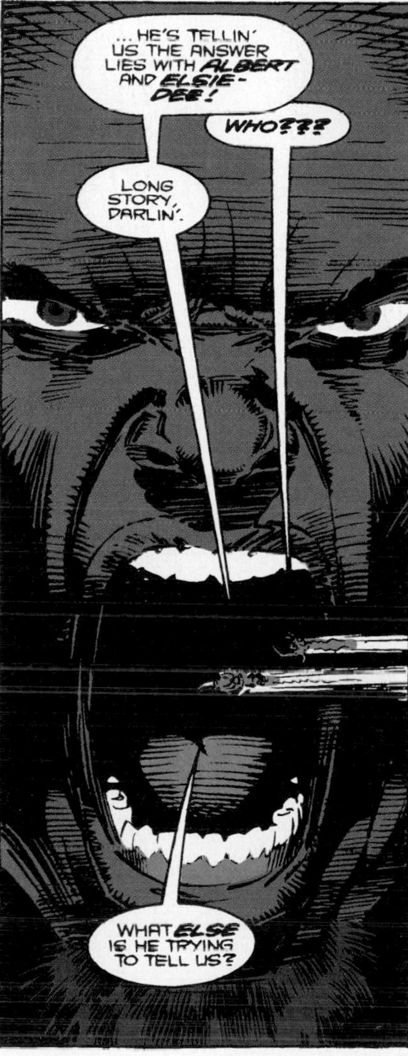
...HE'S TELLIN' US THE ANSWER LIES WITH ALBERT AND ELSIE-DEE!
WHO???
LONG STORY, DARLIN'.
WHAT ELSE IS HE TRYING TO TELL US?

CRUISE MISSILE!
IT'S JUST A PROJECTION, BUT HE GOT THE MESSAGE ACROSS!
BUT WHAT DOES A MISSILE HAVE TO DO WITH ALBERT AND ELSIE-DEE?

WE'VE BEEN NUKED!
IT WAS JUST AN AMAZIN' SIMULATION, DARLIN'-- JUST LIKE THE MISSILE!
IT HAD ALL THE WAVE CHARACTERISTICS OF AN ANTI-MATTER IMPLOSION!
A REAL ONE MIGHT TRIGGER A CHAIN RE-ACTION THAT COULD INITIATE THE CRUNCH!
GATEWAY'S IMAGE IS GONE! LIKE SOMEBODY TURNED HIM OFF...!
...AND THAT SOMEBODY IS MORE THAN LIKELY, MOJO!
SO-- WHAT SHALL IT BE, JUBILEE?
YOUR WORTHLESS FREEDOM IN EXCHANGE FOR WOLVERINE'S LIFE?
THE REST OF YOUR BORING, USELESS EXISTENCE IN TRADE FOR THE CONTINUANCE OF EVERYTHING FOR ETERNITY??
UHH, CAN I THINK ABOUT THIS FOR A SEC?
TIME'S A WASTING, CHILD!
SIC 'EM, WRAITHS!!

THIS IS JUST STALLIN' FOR TIME--
--AND TIME IS RUNNIN' OUT!

CATCH, SPIRAL!
YOU TWO GO BACK AND FETCH THAT MISSILE!
BUT, WHAT--?

I'LL FIGURE OUT WHAT TO DO WITH IT, WHEN I GET IT!
JUST GET VORTEXIN' AND FIND THAT CUTE LITTLE ANDROID AND HER GOOD-LOOKIN' PAL!

SPIRAL! YOU CAN'T RUN OUT ON MY WOLVIE!

SHE DID THE RIGHT THING, JUBILEE.
A LOT MORE AT STAKE HERE THAN JUST THE OL' CANUCKLEHEAD...

...LIKE EVERYTHIN' THAT EVER WAS AND EVER WILL BE!

SCHUCK

SCHRAK!

WOLVIE'S GONNA GO THROUGH YOUR WRAITHS LIKE A BALONEY-SLICER ON "HIGH," MOJO!

AND HE'LL NEVER DEPLETE MY STOCK, MY SOON-TO-BE-THRALL!

WRAITHS ARE AS EGREGIOUSLY PLENTIFUL, PREDATORY AND CHEAP AS ACTORS!

CANADA.
THAT'S IT!
HOW'D YOU FIND IT SO FAST?
SPIWAL!
PIERCE BUILT THESE TWO ANDROIDS WITH BODY SHOP COMPONENTS. I IMBED A TRACER IN ALL MY WORK!
LET'S GET STARTED BEFORE WE START TO FORGET--
GRRRRR!
FORGET?
OF COURSE! YOU CAN'T RETAIN MEMORIES OF THE FUTURE!
BZT!
WEGGO MY FACE!
BACK OFF!
YOU TAWDWY TWOWWOPS AWEN'T DOING DIDDWY WITH MY CWUISE MISSILE UNTIL I FIND OUT WHAT'S TWANSPIWING HERE!
WE NEED YOUR MISSILE TO SAVE WOLVERINE IN THE FAR FUTURE!
THAT DOESN'T TWACK!
IF WOLVEWINE IS IN DANGER IN THE FUTURE, HOW COME HE'S DEAD IN THE PAST?
OH, THAT THING! THAT'S JUST A RELIC FROM AN ALTERNATE TIME STRING, BUT IF IT'S SO IMPORTANT TO YOU, I'LL SEND YOU BACK TO UNRAVEL IT...
...BUT FIRST YOU HAND OVER THE MISSILE! DEAL?

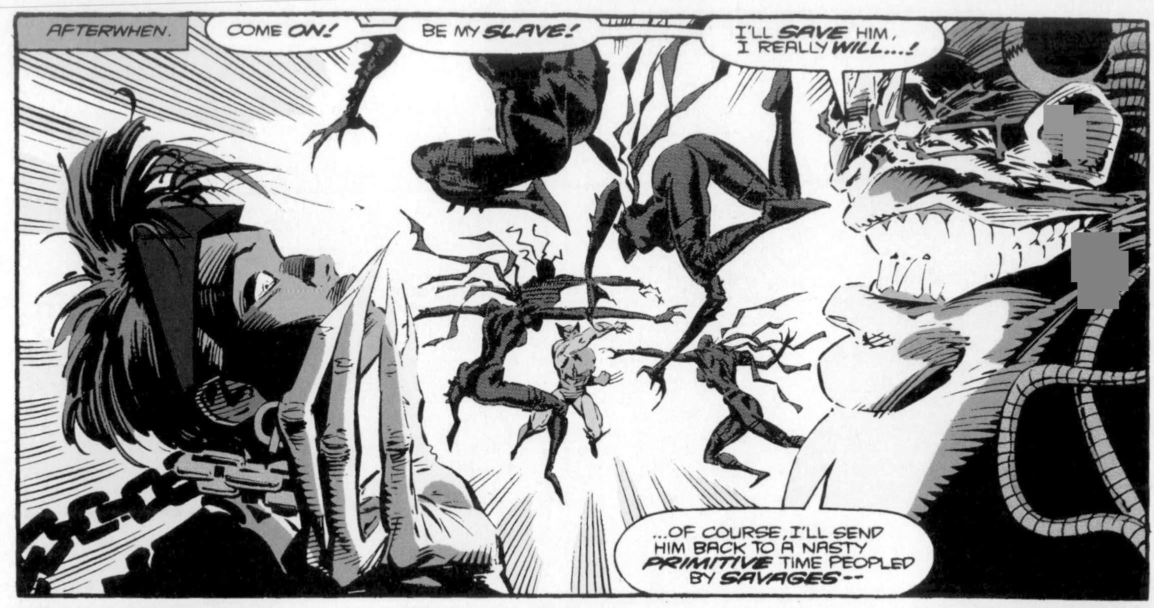
AFTERWHEN.
COME ON!
BE MY SLAVE!
I'LL SAVE HIM, I REALLY WILL...!
...OF COURSE, I'LL SEND HIM BACK TO A NASTY PRIMITIVE TIME PEOPLED BY SAVAGES--

SHOOOOM!
HA.
THE LADIES CAME THROUGH FOR ME!

CANADA.
...WE SENT THE MISSILE AHEAD AND WE SENT THE TWO ANDROIDS AND THEIR FRIEND BACK--
-- BUT WHY DID WE DO THAT? WHY DID I LEAVE THE VORTEX TO THE FUTURE OPEN?
IS THIS CLAWED SKELETON THE REMAINS OF WHO WE THINK IT IS?

I'M SURE WE KNEW ALL THESE THINGS, BUT THE MEMORIES ARE FADING LIKE LAST NIGHT'S DREAMS!
THE MORE I GRASP FOR THEM, THE FASTER THEY WAFT AWAY--
--GONE!
THEY WERE DREAMS, MYSTIQUE...

...DREAMS ABOUT THE FUTURE!
SCHLICK!
CAN'T HAVE THIS BAD GUY GO ZOOMIN' AROUND ANY OL' PLACE!
GOTTA MAKE THIS COUNT LIKE THE LAST SHOT IN A GAME O' EIGHT-BALL...
...GOTTA CALL THE POCKET I AIM TO SINK!
GUESS WHAT, MOJO?
YOU'RE IT!
YOU'RE BLUFFING!
WHAT ABOUT JUBILEE?
WHAT ABOUT YOURSELF??
IF WE DON'T STOP YOU, EVERYTHING WE EVER DID WILL NEVER HAVE BEEN...
...I RECKON SOME O' THOSE GOOD TIMES WERE WORTH THIS!
'SIDES--YOU SURE AIN'T OFFERIN' ANY ALTERNATIVES, IF YOU CATCH MY DRIFT!

HE'S GOING TO RADICALLY DIS-CORPORATE US--!
SAVE HIM!
SAVE YOUR-SELF!
BUT MOST IMPORTANT OF ALL...
SAVE ME, YOU LITTLE--
GET REAL, MOJO...!
...AND CHOMP A TIC-TAC WHILE YOU'RE AT IT!
SHE DISAPPEARED! DID I DO THAT?
AGGGGH! WHO DID YOU THINK DID IT, THE TOOTH FAIRY?
SHE WAS FROM A TIME-STRING WHERE YOU WERE COMPLIANT!!
NOW WE'RE ALL DOOMED!
MUST'VE HIT HIS WHINE-CENTER...
HEY, NO MORE CHAIN-CITY!
I'M OUT OF HERE!
CANADA.
...NOW WHY DID I LEAVE THIS LITTLE VORTEX OPEN? WHO OR WHAT WAS SUPPOSED TO COME THROUGH IT?
MAYBE YOU SHOULD REDIRECT IT SOMEPLACE WHERE THEY HAVE THE FACILITIES TO DEAL WITH THE UN-KNOWN!
SAY, WASN'T THERE A SKELETON OVER THERE JUST A SECOND AGO?
GOOD IDEA--

THAT OTHER WHEN.
THESE LEATHER ZOMBIES THE BEST YOU CAN TROT OUT, MOJO?
THEY AIN'T HARDLY WORTH THE TROUBLE O' EXTRUDIN' THE ADAMANTIUM!
SCRHEKK!

...THE MISSILE CAME OUT OF THAT COSMIC TWISTER--
--SO IT MUST BE A DOORWAY BACK TO OUR OWN TIME!
OOOOOOH, GOTTA TIME THIS JUST RIGHT!

I DON'T NEED THOSE UNGRATEFUL TIME-DANCERS TO MAGICK MY WAY BACK OUT OF HARM'S WAY!
I CAN TIME-SHIFT MYSELF JUST LIKE THAT!
SNAP!
ACK!
ALMOST HAD IT THAT TIME!
NOT ENOUGH PHASE CONTROL--
SPAK!
CUT!
DON'T RECORD THIS, YOU SPHEROID-DROID--!
HEADS UP, MOJO!

URK! URK! URK!
SO WHAT'S IT GONNA BE?
A CLAW SANDWICH OR A FACE-FULL O' CRUISE MISSILE?
BZT!
LET'S TALK DEAL!
HOWABOUT A POINT SHARE ON THE HOLO-VISION GROSS!
8% OF ANCILLARY LICENSING!!!
I'LL GIVE YOU EIGHT PERCENT--!
TIME TO GO, WOLVIE!
...EARTH TO WOLVERINE! EARTH TO WOLVERINE--!

--WAKE UP, STUMPY!
YER BULLETS JUST GOT BUMPED!
BULLETS?

RIGHT. YER ACES IS THE HIGH PAIR SHOWIN' BUT THE HAIRCUT JUST RAISED YOU A BUCK FIFTY.
C'EST VRAI, MY FRIEND. ONE HUNDRED FIFTY DOLLARS TO STAY IN.
EVERYBODY ELSE IS SEEING HIM. YOU CALLING HIS BLUFF, TOO?

TELEPHONE CALL FOR YOU, WOLVERINE!
IT'S FROM JUBILEE. COLLECT. XAVIER TRANSFERRED IT HERE FROM THE ACADEMY...
FIGGERS.
'SCUSE ME, GENTS--
DON'T GET LOST, MON AMI-- NOT WHEN YOU OWE ME A COOL FIVE THOUSAND!
FIVE LARGE?
I MUST'VE BEEN IN ANOTHER DIMENSION!

WHAT'S THE PROB, DARLIN'? YA KNOW-- I WAS JUST THINKIN' ABOUT YOU ...
...BUT I HAD SOME SORT O' WEIRD MEMORY LAPSE OR SOMETHIN'--
GEE, THAT'S REALLY NICE AND ALL THAT...

...AND I'VE BEEN HAVING MEMORY PROBLEMS TOO, BUT RIGHT NOW I'M IN A *TEENSY* LITTLE BIT OF TROUBLE, AND COULD YOU *PLEEEEEASE* COME OVER AND BAIL ME OUT--

BAIL YOU OUT?

JUST *WHAT* DID THE COPS *NAB* YOU FOR, *JUBILEE?*

UHHH, DRIVING WITHOUT A LICENSE, SPEEDING, RESISTING ARREST--OH, AND *CUSTOMS* ZAPPED ME BECAUSE YOUR STUPID MOTORCYCLE DIDN'T HAVE AN IMPORT DUTY STAMP!

IMPORT DUTY???

THAT'S A *MADE IN THE USA HARLEY FREAKIN' DAVIDSON...!*

I DON'T OWE ANY *IMPORT DUTY* ON THAT BIKE!

YEAH, WELL, YOU *DO* IF THE BIKE'S IN *TOKYO,* DUDE!

THE END

WOLVERINE #53, PAGE 1 ART BY MARC SILVESTRI & DAN GREEN

MARVEL COMICS
WOLVERINE
AND NOW--
SHATTERSTAR!
© 1992 MARVEL ENT. GROUP, INC.
$1.75 US
$2.15 CAN
54
MAY
CC 02254
APPROVED BY THE COMICS CODE AUTHORITY

STAN LEE PRESENTS:
STATION IDENTIFICATION
THE SOUTH BRONX, NEW YORK.
GET BACK HERE, Y'MORLOCK DIRTBAG!
LOOKITEM' HOBBLIN'!
C'MERE AN' PLAY, YA MUTIE FREAK!
FABIAN NICIEZA GUEST WRITER
DARICK ROBERTSON GUEST PENCILER
DON HUDSON GUEST INKER
BROSSEAU + HEISLER LETTERERS
KELLY CORVESE COLORIST
BOB HARRAS EDITOR
TOM DEFALCO EDITOR IN CHIEF

NO
PLEASE, NO
PLEASE
AH--!
NICE REACTION SHOT.
WELCOME TO TONIGHT'S *SHOW,* MUTIE.
WHAT SAY WE MAKE IT ONE THE FOLKS AT HOME'RE GONNA ENJOY.
WHAT--? WHY--?
RUN, MUTIE! RUN FOR YOUR LIFE!

RUNS LIKE A WALRUS! ON 'IM, LINK!
CHINK
CUEBALL NAILS THE NOGGIN'!
UHNFF--!
GEEK ALERT! THIS AIN'T ONE FOR THE RERUNS, GANG!
PLEASE-- WHY--
WHY? WHY?! HEY GUYS-- WHY?
BECAUSE ENTERTAINMENT'S IN OUR BLOOD!
NOW YOUR BLOOD'S IN OUR ENTERTAINMENT!
JESTE

--VIDEOTAPE WAS DELIVERED TO EYE-WITNESS NEWS AN HOUR AGO--
--ONCE AGAIN SHOWING THE GRAPHIC MURDER OF AN UNIDENTIFIED MUTANT--
--BY THE GANG WHO CALL THEMSELVES THE VIDKIDS.
THIS BRINGS TO FOUR THE NUMBER OF FILMED MURDERS COMMITTED BY THIS GANG THROUGHOUT THE FIVE BOROUGHS.
BURN MUTIE SCUM
I find the actions undertaken by these people to be UN-SETTLING--but INTRIGUING.
Save for AMERICAN GLADIATORS, it is as CLOSE a use of the televised medium of THIS world--
--to the kinds of programming I grew up with on MY home-world.
My name is SHATTER-STAR. I am a stranger to the ways of this Earth.
But not a stranger to the ways of these Vidkids.
COMPUTER--PLEASE DIS-PLAY ASSAULT LOCATIONS.

Two in the place called the Bronx. One in Queens. One in Manhattan.
No discernible pattern, save for the fact those hunted and killed were ALL mutants.
Or more precisely, MORLOCKS.
Mutants who have ISOLATED themselves from society due to their deformities or disfigurements.
SHATTER-- PLANNIN' A WORKOUT SESSION? AH'LL JOIN YOU.
SAM GUTHRIE. A fellow member of the X-FORCE unit I have allied myself with.
He is a good man, but he wouldn't understand why I need to find these Vidkids.
NO, GUTHRIE.
TONIGHT, I DO NOT PLAN TO PRACTICE...
...I PLAN TO HUNT!
BUTTON

XAVIER'S SCHOOL FOR GIFTED YOUNGSTERS IN SALEM CENTER, NEW YORK.
...A PLACE WHICH ISN'T WHAT IT APPEARS TO BE FROM THE OUTSIDE...
HEADS UP, WOLVIE!
TYRANNOSAUR CAME UP OUTTA NOWHERE!
PART OF THE SAVAGE LAND PROGRAM, DARLIN'.
GOTTA BE PREPARED ALL THE TIME--
--AND WORK THROUGH WHAT-EVER COMES UP!
SHREKSH

FINE, YOU JUST KEEP ON HAVIN' FUN--
--BUT THE MISSION OP IS TO REACH THE CAVE AN' RESCUE WHO-EVER'S IN--
--SIDE--?
MAGNETO?!
OOMPH
STUPID!
STUPID!
STUPID!
AH KNOW IT'S JUST A CONSTRUCT PRO-GRAMMED T'SIMULATE MAGNETO'S POWERS, BUT I STILL CHOKED!
SHREKSHKT
LIKE I SAID, ROGUE ...
...GOTTA BE PREPARED FOR ANY CONTINGENCY.
COMPUTER --END PROGRAM.

YEAH, YEAH... AH KNOW.
JUST WASN'T EXPECTIN' MAGNETO, THAT'S ALL.
STILL CARRYIN' THE TORCH FOR HIM?
NO!
AH DON'T KNOW HOW AH FEEL ABOUT HIM.
DON'T LET IT THROW YOU OFF.
WHAT'S THROWIN' ME OFF IS YOU LECTURIN' ME ON DANGER ROOM ETI-QUETTE!
AH ALWAYS THOUGHT YOU WERE THE ONE WHO CALLED THESE PRACTICE SESSIONS A WASTE OF TIME.
ONLY WHEN I DON'T WIN THEM.
OH, NICE ATTITUDE!
SNAPT

THE ONLY ATTITUDE I'VE EVER KNOWN.
"WHATEVER GETS YOU THROUGH THE NIGHT."
THAT'S A LITTLE TOO COMFORTABLE FOR ME, LOGAN.

CHECK THE NEWS OUT. HEARD O' THESE GUYS YET?
BUNCHA KIDS HUNTIN' MORLOCKS.
HUNTIN' FOR SPORT. FOR FUN.
NEITHER ONE'S A REASON TO HUNT.
MAN OR ANIMAL...

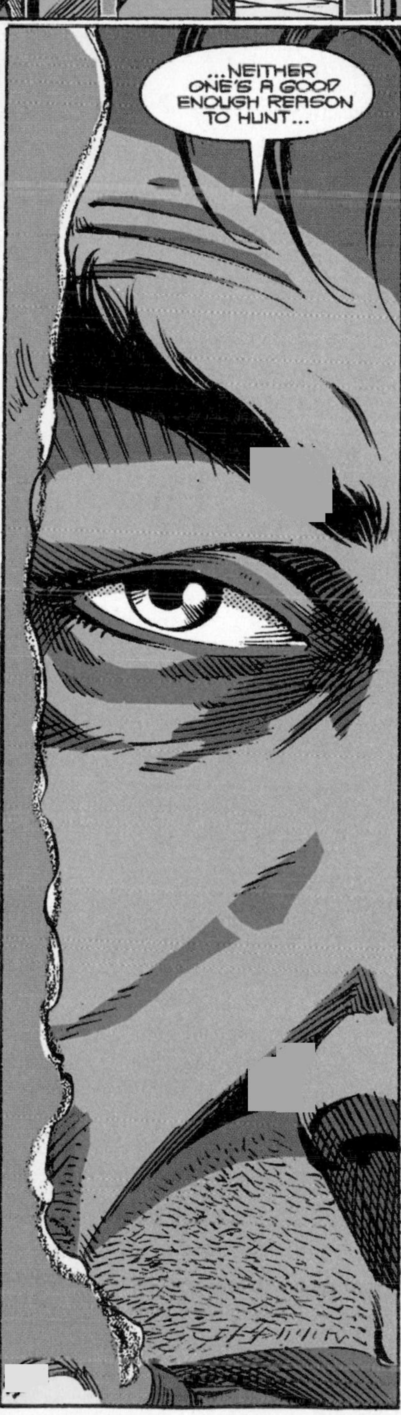
...NEITHER ONE'S A GOOD ENOUGH REASON TO HUNT...

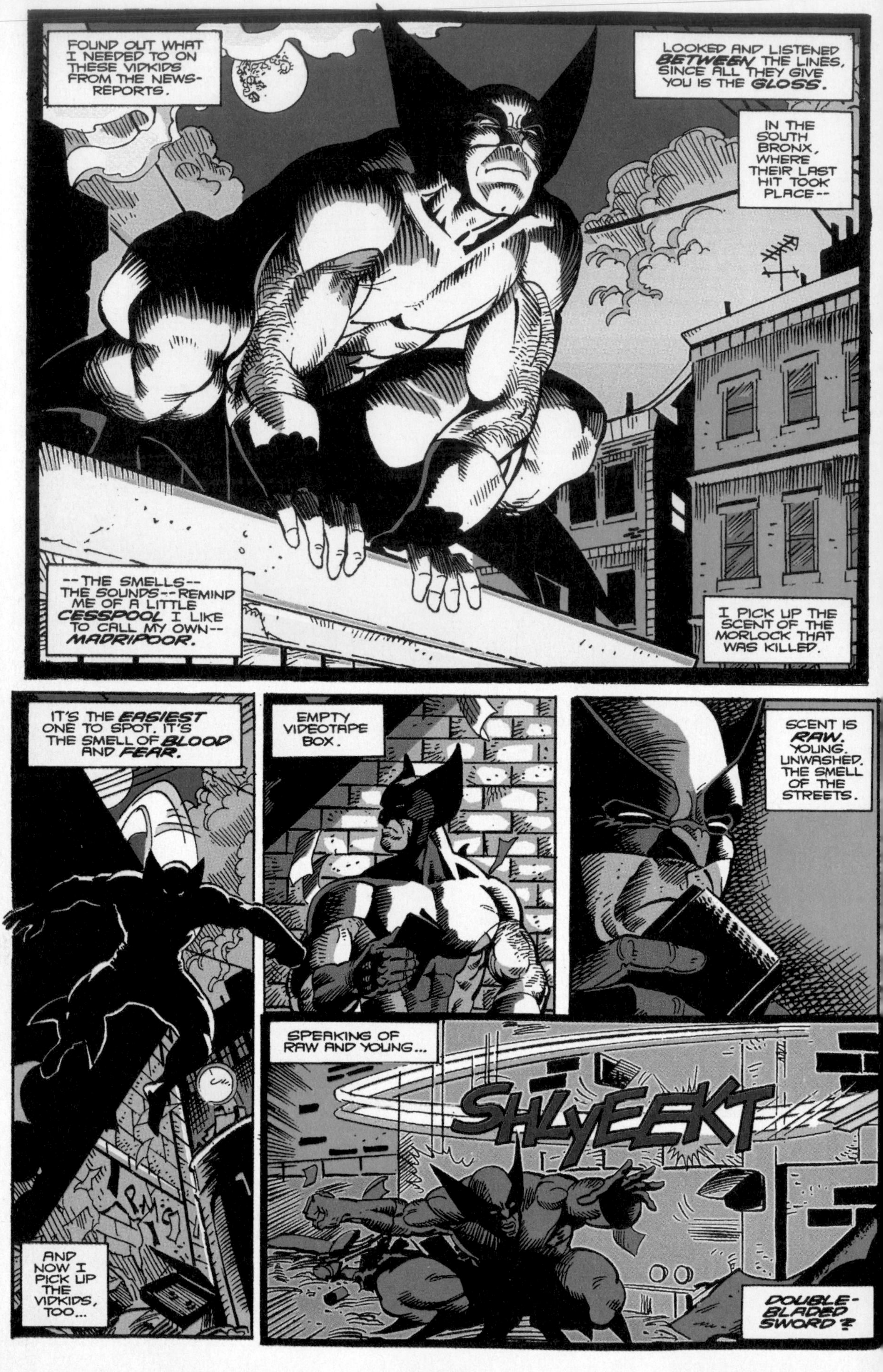

FOUND OUT WHAT I NEEDED TO ON THESE VIDKIDS FROM THE NEWS-REPORTS.

LOOKED AND LISTENED *BETWEEN* THE LINES, SINCE ALL THEY GIVE YOU IS THE *GLOSS*.

IN THE SOUTH BRONX, WHERE THEIR LAST HIT TOOK PLACE--

--THE SMELLS-- THE SOUNDS--REMIND ME OF A LITTLE *CESSPOOL* I LIKE TO CALL MY OWN-- *MADRIPOOR*.

I PICK UP THE SCENT OF THE MORLOCK THAT WAS KILLED.

IT'S THE *EASIEST* ONE TO SPOT. IT'S THE SMELL OF *BLOOD* AND *FEAR*.

AND NOW I PICK UP THE VIDKIDS, TOO...

EMPTY VIDEOTAPE BOX.

SCENT IS *RAW*. YOUNG. UNWASHED. THE SMELL OF THE STREETS.

SPEAKING OF RAW AND YOUNG...

SHLYEEKT

DOUBLE-BLADED SWORD?

COME OUT OF THE SHADOWS, MURDERER!
STAND IN THE SPOT-LIGHT AND STARE DEATH IN THE FACE!
A VIDKID?
SNIKT
DON'T KNOW FOR SURE...
...DOESN'T FEEL RIGHT, THOUGH.
GOOD MOVE.
THE GANG I'M LOOKIN' FOR ARE PACK-TRAVEL-ERS--
--THIS KID'S SOLO--
--DANGEROUS, BUT SOLO...

ZA'S VID!!
SHRAK
WHO ARE YOU--?
KID'S A TALKER. STUPID.
THWUMP
CHIKT
NOT BAD. ALMOST BROKE A SWEAT.
YOU REALLY AIN'T INTERESTED IN SEEIN' THE MIDDLE FINGER, ARE YOU?

CLAWS--?
YOU ARE-- YOU--
LORD WOLVERINE
WARRIOR OF LEGEND!
ARENA WARRIOR SHATTERSTAR OFFERS HIS SWORD TO YOU.
MY LIFE IS FORFEIT SHOULD YOU WISH, FOR DISHONORING YOU IN CARELESS COMBAT.
I'M STARTIN' T'LIKE THIS KID.
HEY... GET UP...
GOT YOUR SCENT NOW.
YOU'RE ONE OF CABLE'S NEW ONES? X-FORCE BRAT?
I CAN SMELL HIM ON YOU.
WHAT'S YOUR STAKE IN ALL OF THIS?
ON MY WORLD, ARENA SPORT FOR ENTERTAIN-MENT IS OUR WAY OF LIFE.
THE SITUATION INTRIGUED ME. I SOUGHT TO PLAY IN THEIR GAME.
THIS AIN'T A GAME, KID.
I'M HERE TO PUT A STOP TO IT.
WHYEVER FOR?
COME WITH ME AN' FIND OUT.
YOU KNOW WHERE THEY ARE?
I GOT A SCENT. AN' I KNOW WHERE THE MORLOCK'S MAIN TUNNELS ARE.

WE RIDE THE *6 TRAIN* TO THE BROOKLYN BRIDGE.

THE MORLOCK TUNNELS THAT LEAD TO THE CATACOMBS UNDER THE CITY ARE JUST A FEW BLOCKS AWAY.

THE KID'S TENSE. MAYBE NERVOUS 'CAUSE OF ME.

MAYBE 'CAUSE THIS HITS TOO CLOSE TO HOME FOR HIM.

EITHER WAY, WE GOT A JOB TO DO...

MAR

WHO KNEW? *WHO? STREISAND?* BEST DIRECTOR? *FEH!*

BELINDA CARUSO IS COOL

Creek

Creek

Creek

K-SCOPE, STAY HERE AN' WATCH THE TUNNELS.
GET A NICE PAN SHOT AS WE COME BACK WITH THE KILLS.
INTO THE DARK FANTASTIC! YEEEHAA!
BACK TO THE WALL! MASADA DEFENSE!
HOPELESS SITCH. GREAT EMOTIONAL PATHOS.
AUDIENCE'LL REALLY IDENTIFY WITH THE VICTIM NOW.
HUH--?
HEH-HEH. NEVER GIVE AN AWARD T'THE BEST BOY!

VIDKIDS FOCUS! WE'RE IN TROUBLE!!
GOT THAT RIGHT.
We face them side-by-side. It is an HONOR.
But our opponents remind me so much of my comrades from Mojoworld... too much...
CUEBALL-- LE'S RACK 'M UP!
...is this how OTHERS view us, then?
As ranting LUNATICS with a one-camera point of view?
CLAP CLAP CLAP
DUMPED ON THE REST, NOW TRY THE BEST!

OLIVER STONE AN' JOHN FORD WRAPPED INTO ONE.
"AND THE OSCAR GOES TO..."
US!
WHY?
THE PSYCHO HUNT I CAN FIGURE OUT, BUT WHY MUTANTS?
WHY NOT, CLAWS?
MAKES FOR BETTER SOUND BITES, RIGHT?
SO IT COULD HAVE BEEN BLACKS? OR JEWS? GAYS?
COULDA BEEN GIRL SCOUTS, BUT MUTIES SUFFICE.
GIRL SCOUTS AIN'T A BAD IDEA, THOUGH.
NOT FOR JUSTICE, THEN?
OR HONOR?
OR EVEN FREEDOM?
BETTER THAN THAT, CUTIE--FOR KICKS!!

ENOUGH!
ENOUGH O' THIS MADNESS PLAYED OUT LIKE A GAME.
THEY'RE KIDS--PUNKS--I GAVE 'EM A SHOT--HEARD THEIR STORY, GAVE 'EM A CHANCE--
--BUT NO MORE!
THEY MAY THINK THEY'RE JUST MAKIN' A MOVIE--
--BUT I GET THE FINAL CUT!!
We fight side-by-side again, but it is different this time...
WE AIN'T FIGHTIN' OUT OF SELF-DEFENSE, OR EVEN PRO-TECTIN' ANYONE--
We're fighting out of ANGER.
YOU'RE GOOD, PRETTY BOY.
C'MON, THEN, ONE OF US ENDS UP ON THE CUTTING ROOM FLOOR!
YOU KNOW NOTHING ABOUT THE "CUTTING ROOM FLOOR"
--UNTIL YOU HAVE WALKED THROUGH IT IN THE BLOOD OF YOUR BROTHERS!

YOU BOYS GOTTA LEARN TO LIGHTEN UP!
LET'S FORGET ABOUT ALL THIS AN' PLAY BALL!
THUNK
THAT ACTUALLY HURT.
WAIT'LL THE PUNK GETS A LOAD OF MY FASTBALL.
COME NOW, WOMAN!
WHERE HAS YOUR POSING FOR THE CAMERAS GONE?
YOU ARE A CRUEL REFLECTION OF EVERYTHING I HAVE BEEN MY ENTIRE LIFE!

THAT'S GIVIN' 'EM WHAT THEY WANT--THE ULTIMATE SHOT--THEIR OWN DEATHS FOR THE CAMERA.

WHAT THEN--?

SNIKT

THEY SAY THE BEST WAY TO PUNISH A PUNK...

SHKASH

...IS TO TAKE AWAY HIS TOYS.
It is over then?
The Vidkids have been stopped. Some killed, some hurt, some merely spiritually crushed.
But is it enough to stop their ways?
I do not know, for sure.

KID'S QUIET AS THE COPS ROUND UP THE VIDKIDS.
MEDIA VULTURES SHOW UP. OF COURSE.
KID WATCHES THE CIRCUS, BUT IT'S NOT WITH INNOCENT EYES.
INSTEAD OF SEEIN' 'EM GET SLAPPED AN' CAGED LIKE THEY DESERVE...
...WE WATCH 'EM GET EXACTLY WHAT THEY WANT-- A FORUM FOR THEIR MADNESS.
THIS TELEVISION ON YOUR WORLD -- IT IS STRANGE...
DON'T WATCH TOO MUCH OF IT, MYSELF.
AT ITS WORST, I FIGURE IT'S AN ESCAPE--
--FOR PEOPLE WHO DON'T WANT T' WORK AT MAKIN' THEIR LIVES MEAN ANYTHING.
ON MY WORLD, IT HAS MADE LIFE UNBEARABLE -- ON THIS ONE, TOO LENIENT.
WHERE DO I FIT IN?
WHERE THE REST OF US USUALLY DO.
RIGHT IN THE MIDDLE.
I LEAVE THE KID. HE'S GONNA STAND THERE A WHILE, WATCHING THE VULTURES GO TO WORK.
WONDERIN' HOW MANY PIECES THEY'VE ALREADY TORN OUT OF HIS FLESH...
...AN' IF WHAT THEY'VE LEFT IS ENOUGH TO MAKE UP A WHOLE MAN OR NOT...
END

MARVEL COMICS
WOLVERINE
Featuring
GAMBIT! JUBILEE! SUNFIRE!
© 1992 MARVEL ENT. GROUP, INC.
$1.75 US
$2.15 CAN
55
JUNE
02254
APPROVED BY THE COMICS CODE AUTHORITY
AND INTRODUCING--
THE MADNESS OF
CYLLA!

THIRTY SLASHES OVER TOKYO
OR "SAYONARA YELLOW BRICK ROAD"
BEEEEEEEEEEEEEP!
LOS ANGEL
INTERNATIONAL
FLIGHT 301 TO TOKYO NOW BOARDING PARENTS WITH SMALL CHILDREN AND PASSENGERS IN WHEELCHAIRS AT INTERNATIONAL DEPARTURES, GATE 17...
WOULD YOU MIND STEPPING THIS WAY, SIR?
3A
SET OFF THE METAL-DETECTOR, DID I?
DON'T SUPPOSE YA MAKE EXCEPTIONS FOR MUTANTS, HUH?
DIDN'T THINK SO.
DAT'S OUR FLIGHT DEY CALLIN', LOGAN--
WE'D PREFER TO AVOID A SCENE, SIR...
I HEARD IT, GAMBIT. DON'T HAVE A VACHE...
I'LL CLEAR THIS UP IN A FEW SECONDS...
LARRY HAMA -- SCRIPT
MARC SILVESTRI -- PENCILS
DAN GREEN -- INKS
STEVE BUCCELLATO -- COLORING
PAT BROSSEAU -- LETTERING
BOB HARRAS -- EDITOR
TOM DEFALCO -- EDITOR IN CHIEF

TEN MINUTES LATER...

OKAY, WE GIVE UP...

...WHERE DO YOU HAVE IT STASHED? OUR DETECTORS SHOW OVER *EIGHT POUNDS* OF *METAL* ON YOU! ENOUGH FOR A LARGE *GUN* OR MULTIPLE *GRENADES!*

I AIN'T *PACKIN'*, LADY! IT'S ALL IN THE *BONES*--

THAT DOESN'T FLY. INTERNAL ORTHOPEDIC APPLIANCES LEAVE BIG SURGICAL SCARS AND YOU DON'T HAVE ANY!

WOULD YA BELIEVE I *HEAL* REAL *GOOD?*

TRES DESHABILLE.
YEAH, I FEEL LIKE I BEEN HERE BEFORE, TOO...
WHY DON'T YOU JUS' SKIP ON HOME, GAMBIT? NO REAL USE IN YOU TAGGIN' ALONG ALL THE WAY TO NIPPON!
I T'INK MAYBE I STICK WIT YOU UNTIL YOU PAY UP DAT FI' T'OUSAND YOU OWE ME.*
DON'T SUPPOSE YOU'D TAKE A PARTNERSHIP IN A BAR IN MADRIPOOR, HUH?
*GAMBIT WON IT IN A POKER GAME LAST ISSUE!
TES
2-46
IT IS TO LAUGH, NON?
HA.
WELCOME TO LOS ANGELES INTERNATIONAL AIRPORT
YO, DUDE! YOU FORGOT TO SHAVE YOUR BACK THIS MORNING!
HOLD IT!
AN INTEGRAL PART OF YOUR BODY OR NOT, THE SIX BLADES IN QUESTION CONSTITUTE RETRACTABLE WEAPONS WITH CUTTING EDGES IN EXCESS OF SIX INCHES IN LENGTH AND AS SUCH FALL UNDER THE CODIFIED RESTRICTIONS OF THE AIR TRAVEL SECURITY ACT OF 1972--
WHAT'S THAT IN PLAIN-SPEAK?
YOU'RE NOT FLYING.
THOUGHT SO.
--LAST CALL FOR FLIGHT 301!
MONSIEUR, I T'INK A TELEPHONE CALL TO NICK FURY AT S.H.I.E.L.D. SETTLE DIS' RIGHT UP!

ELSEWHERE...
WAKE UP.
TIME TO REACTIVATE YOUR CONSCIOUSNESS.
WHO--?
I AM THE MAINTENANCE PROGRAM. YOU HAVE BEEN SHUT DOWN TO MINIMALIZE YOUR ENERGY REQUIREMENTS AND MAXIMIZE YOUR SURVIVABILITY.
PIERCE. IS HE--?
--FORMATTED? YES. BEYOND RETRIEVAL. YOU MUST CARRY ON...

GET ME OUT OF THIS--
IN TIME. THE SEARCH PROGRAMS HAVE BEEN BUSY. THE LOGAN FLAG WAS TRIGGERED BY THE MONITOR ON THE AIRLINE COMPUTERS SERVICING THE PACIFIC RIM.
THE WOLVERINE/LOGAN/PATCH FLAG ON THE S.H.I.E.L.D. COMMO-TAP HAS BEEN TRIGGERED!
IT'S A REQUEST FOR A SECURITY WAIVER ON A FLIGHT TO TOKYO FOR A MR. LOGAN!
BRRRING!

ANALOGUE VOICE INCOMING ON LAND-LINE. AUDIO RECEPTORS ON. VOICE SYNTHESIZER ON.
THERE WAS A POWER-DROP ON THE LINE DURING THE S.H.I.E.L.D. TAP! SOMEBODY ELSE WAS LISTENING IN!

I'LL DEAL WITH IT.
YES, YOU WILL. I'M OPENING A CELLULAR LINE. REFORMAT VOICE MODULE TO "IZZY" CONFIG--READY?

EDDIE? THIS IS IZZY AT THE MAIN OFFICE. WE GOT A RE-ROUTE. LADING BILL #506, HARDY CYLINDER CLAMPS & FROMMISTATS IN LONG-TERM STORAGE?
RIGHT. BIG OBLONG, COFFIN-SIZED BOX...
...I REMEMBER BECAUSE IT DIDN'T STACK RIGHT. HADDA LAY IT ACROSS TWO ROWS O' STANDARD MACHINE CRATES.
WHERE'S IT GOIN'?
TAKE IT DOWN TO OVERSEAS AIR-FREIGHT.
506 HARDY CYLINDER CLAMPS & FROMMISTATS
IT'S GOING TO TOKYO--
--THE PAPERWORK WILL FOLLOW.

TOKYO.
ROPONGI DISTRICT STATION OF THE TOKYO METROPOLITAN POLICE.
--I SAID, TAKE YOUR PROTO-PUKE FASHION STATEMENTS OUTTA MY FACE...
...AND TURN DOWN YOUR ATTITUDE CONTROL-KNOB!
<WHAT DID SHE SAY?>*
<WHO CARES?>
<LET'S JUST BEAT HER UP AND TAKE HER STUFF!>
*TRANSLATED FROM JAPANESE.
NO WAY!
I KNOW WHAT THAT MEANS IN ANY LANGUAGE!
PAF
PAF
PAF
PAF
PAF
MATRON!!
I NEED TO GET A MESSAGE OUT OF HERE!>
<SO DOES EVERYBODY ELSE!>
<EVERYBODY ELSE ISN'T TRYING TO REACH THE HAND!>

NARITA AIRPORT, TOKYO.
YOU KNOW HOW TO HAIL A TAXI IN JAPANESE, MON AMI?
SURE.
TA-K'SHI!
SKREEEEEEE
IT'S ALL NUANCE AND INFLECTION, N'EST-CE-PAS?
GET'S RESULTS.
<LINE JUMPER!!>
I AM SO PLEASED TO SERVING YOU, GENTLEMENS! PLEASE TO ME SAY DESTINATION IN ENGLISH, WHICH I ARE EXCELLENTLY UNDERSTAND AS YOU CAN SEE!
ROPONGI DISTRICT POLICE STATION.
<LOW-BORN DOG! THAT WAS MY FARE! I AM CALLING THE TAXI MINISTRY-->
POLICE STATION! I ARE KNOW VERY WELL! PLEASE GET IN!
CLUNCH!
HEY! YOU'RE HEADIN' FOR THE WRONG EXIT! ROPONGI IS IN THE OTHER DIRECTION, BUB!
PLEASE TO SIT BACK! THIS SHORT-CUT! VERY FAST. MUCH SAVING OF TIME!
SKREEEEE!

SHORT-CUT.
RIGHT.
THROUGH A CAR-WASH?
MAYBE THE DRIVER FIGGERS TO LOSE "FACE" IF HE SHOWS AT THE COP-SHOP WITH A DUSTY RIDE.
MAYBE, HIS UNCLE SABURO OWNS THE CAR-WASH.
MAYBE THIS IS A SET-UP!
SHUK! SHUK!
WE'VE BEEN SET-UP!
DO TELL!
SNIKT!
SNIKT!

I'M OPENING WITH A PAIR O' TRAYS, GAMBIT--
--THAT'S SIX CLAWS TO YOU!
SCHREEEK!
I CALL.
WHATCHA HOLDIN'?
THOOOM!
FULL HOUSE. ACES OVER.
BLOWS THEM AWAY.
THEY FROM THE HAND?
THEY SURE AIN'T FROM THE FOOT.
YOU DON' BE NEEDIN' DIS, MY FRAN!
LIKE WE WAS SAYIN'--
--ROPONGI POLICE STATION, AN' PUT YER FLIP-FLOP TO THE METAL!
YESSIR, MR. GAIJIN!
THAT'S GAIJIN-SAMA, TO YOU, BUB!
< --I HAVE IT ON GOOD AUTHORITY THAT LOGAN IS HERE IN JAPAN...>

<...I CERTAINLY HOPE THAT THIS ODIOUS INDIVIDUAL WASN'T SUMMONED HERE TO OPPOSE THE HAND'S TAKEOVER OF CERTAIN UNDER-WORLD ACTIVITIES!>

<I WOULD BE FORCED TO MAKE THINGS MORE UNPLEASANT THAN THEY AL-READY ARE!>
<YOU PRESUME TOO MUCH, TSURAYABA MATSUO!>
<YOU WILL ADDRESS ME AS "LORD", INSOLENT WENCH!>

<THE HEAD OF THE CLAN YOSHIDA CALLS NO MERE NINJA-MONGER "LORD"!>
<FOR YOUR INFORMATION, MY BETROTHED KNOWS IT IS INAPPROPRIATE FOR HIM TO BE IN JAPAN UNTIL I HAVE FULFILLED MY PLEDGE TO DIVEST THE YOSHIDA CLAN OF ALL DISHONORABLE INTERESTS!>

<FURTHERMORE, THIS BUSINESS BETWEEN CLAN YOSHIDA AND THE HAND HAS NOTHING TO DO WITH LOGAN. YOU HAVE MY WORD ON THAT!>
<IF WE HAVE ANY-THING FURTHER TO DISCUSS, IT SHALL BE OVER CROSSED SWORDS!>
<HE IS BLOWING SMOKE, MARIKO OYABUN...!>
<MATSUO WAS CALLING FROM A CELLULAR PHONE, BUT WE ARE RUNNING A SYSTEM CODE DE-SCRAMBLER AND A SATELLITE-TRACE ON IT!>

<...THAT DOG-EATER, MATSUO, HAS OTHER REASONS FOR WANTING THE LIFE OF LOGAN!>
<MEANWHILE, THE HAND HAS THE YOSHIDAS LIVING IN A STATE OF SIEGE, TRYING TO FORCE US INTO THEIR THRALL!>
<IF LOGAN REALLY IS HERE, HE WOULD BE A POWERFUL ALLY-->
<THAT IS NOT FOR YOU TO SAY!>
<I CANNOT ACCEPT THE LOVE OR HELP OF LOGAN UNTIL I HAVE RE-STORED THE HONOR OF OUR CLAN!>
<THE SATELLITE TRACE CAME IN, MARIKO-OYABUN...>
<"...IT'S JUST OUTSIDE A CAR-WASH NEAR ROPONGI!">
<WE HAVE FAILED YOU, LORD-- IS IT YOUR WISH THAT WE SPILL OUR ENTRAILS IN ATONEMENT?>
<MY DISPLEASURE IS NOT SUCH THAT I WILL REQUIRE YOUR DISEMBOWELMENT, YET...>
<I TRUST YOU DISPATCHED THE POISONER TO TAKE CARE OF THE BRAT?>
<IT WAS DONE AS YOU COMMANDED, OH LORD!>
<SHALL WE INITIATE THE CONTINGENCY PLAN FOR THE GAIJIN LOGAN?>
<BY ALL MEANS.>

AT THE POLICE STATION...
<--NASTY LITTLE FOREIGN-BORN TROUBLE-MAKER! NOW YOU'RE IN FOR IT!>
<YOU'VE BEEN TRANSFERRED TO THE INCORRIGIBLE MINOR FACILITY! THEY DON'T MESS AROUND DOWN THERE!>
YOU TALKIN' TO ME?
ME NO HABLO--ARE WE GOING FOR A RIDE OR WHAT?
30
<SHUT UP AND GET IN!>
THIS IS THE WORST--!
SLAM
--UHH, HI! YOU SPEAK ENGLISH?
YES.
IS THAT EVER A RELIEF! MY NAME'S JUBILEE!
I AM CALLED REIKO.
THIS IS THE PLACE, GAMBIT! WHY DON'T YOU CONVINCE OL' SUSHI-FOR-BRAINS TO STAY PUT WHILE WE COLLECT JUBILEE!
E'COUTER, COCHON! DON' MOVE!
BONK

<...SHE CAUSED A DISTURBANCE. WE LIKE ORDER.>
<HOWABOUT LETTIN' ME HAVE MY BIKE-->
--THAT WILL NOT BE POSSIBLE, MR. LOGAN...!
HAVE YOU GIRLS BEEN BAD?
THAT'S WHEN WE'RE GOOD!
...YOUR DELINQUENCY IN PAYING IMPORT DUTIES ON MOTOR-CYCLE--
--HAS ALERTED MY OFFICE TO YOUR OTHER EGREGIOUS VIOLATIONS!
MY CARD!
JOTARO ISUZU
FIRST ASSISTANT DEPU
INSPECTOR, MINISTRY OF
TRADE, DEPARTMENT OF
ARIFFS AND IMPORT DUTIES
FORCEMENT SECTION.
YOU WOULDN'T BE LYING, WOULD YOU?

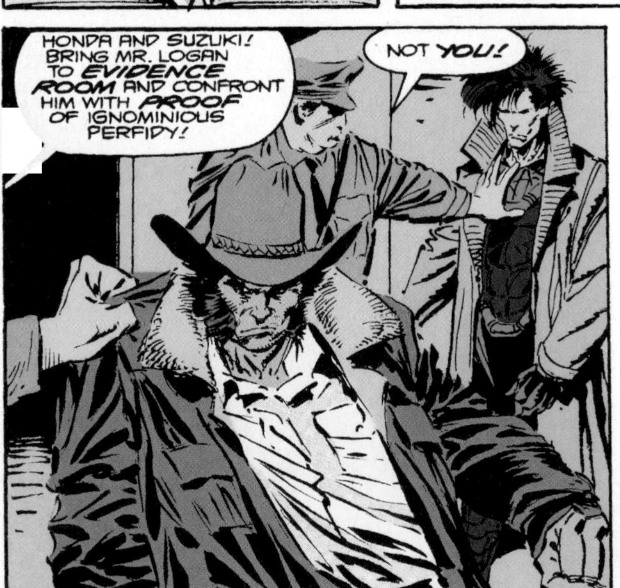

RAYCO? WHAT A TOTALLY COOL NAME!
SOUNDS LIKE AN AUTO-PARTS COMPANY!
UH, LIKE-- WHAT ARE YOU IN FOR?

MURDER.
OH. THAT'S-- INTERESTING.
WHO DID YOU...UMM...
KILL?
A YAKUZA CHIEF. AN EVIL OYABUN NAMED DAI-KUMO.* I DIDN'T KNOW HE WAS A PAWN OF THE HAND...
* WOLVERINE #33!

...MY RASH ACTION INCURRED A TERRIBLE OBLIGATION, WHICH I MUST REPAY. I'M SORRY!
SHHHH!
DON'T BE AFRAID. THE BLADE IS COATED WITH BLOWFISH TOXIN. THE END WILL BE SWIFT--

NO WAY!!

THIS OUGHTA FRY YOUR RETINAS!
PAF!
CAN'T STICK ME IF YOU CAN'T SEE ME!
I NEVER COULD SEE YOU.
MATSUO HAD MY CORNEAS REMOVED BY LASER-SURGERY.
THAT'S THE PRICE OF YOUR LIFE, GIRL. I KILL YOU...
...I GET MY EYES BACK!

SNIP!
-- I'VE NEVER SEEN THIS CRATE BEFORE IN MY LIFE...!
BE THAT AS IT MAY, IT WAS DELIVERED TO NARITA AIRPORT VIA EXPRESS AIR-FREIGHT, ADDRESSED FOR PERSONAL PICK-UP BY YOU!
IT CONTAINS NOT ONLY TAXABLE GOODS, BUT ITEMS SPECIFICALLY ON THE PROHIBITED LIST!
I'M TELLIN' YOU, JOE --
YOU KNOW WHAT'S IN THAT THING?
< GET THE CROW-BAR! >
THE MINISTRY IS NOT NAIVE! WE X-RAYED THIS CRATE!
PROTO-SENTIENT BIOLOGICAL CONSTRUCTS ARE NOT ALLOWED!
A CYBORG??
WHAT ELSE IS IN THERE?
506 HARDY CYLINDER CLAMPS &
A SUB-MINIATURE TELE-COMMUNICATIONS ARRAY, NAV-SAT CONSOLE, A CRYOGENIC DIALYSIS SUITE --
IS IT ACTIVATED?
SCHRACK
WELL, THAT ANSWERS THAT!

< FORGET ABOUT HIM...! >
< ...LOOK WHO JUST WALKED IN!! >
WASN'T NO PROBLEM UNTIL YOU SHOWED UP. WHO ARE YOU?
SHURO YOSHIDA -- CALLED SUNFIRE. AND YOU, ...?
'DEY CALL ME GAMBIT, AN X-MAN, F'R BETTER OR WORSE.
AND YOU DARE TO BRANDISH YOUR WEAPON AT ME, GAMBIT?
IT HAS COME TO MY ATTENTION THAT THERE IS A PRO- BLEM HERE CONCERNING MY ALLIES, THE X-MEN --
NOT AT YOU, MON AMI --
-- AT THAT SMALL ARMY OF NINJAS CREEPING IN BEHIND YOU!

IT IS POINT-LESS TO RESIST --
--IT IS JUST A MATTER OF TIME BEFORE MY BLADE CUTS YOU AND THE POISON TAKES EFFECT!
PAF
PAF
I'LL TAKE MY CHANCES--!
--AND GET A FEW LICKS IN MYSELF!
THWACK!
EVEN IF YOU DO GET LUCKY AND ≡GULP≡ STOP MY CLOCK--
...MY PAL WOLVIE WILL JUST TRACK YOU DOWN!
I'LL CUT HIM, TOO!
ONLY IF YOU CAN GET PAST HIS ADA-MANTIUM CLAWS!
CLAWS?
WHAT ABOUT CLAWS?
THIS "WOLVY", IS HE ALSO CALLED PATCH OR LOGAN?

I KNEW I COULD GET TO YOU BY TRUSTING IN THE EFFICIENCY OF JAPANESE BUREAU-CRATS!
--AND THEY TRACKED YOU RIGHT DOWN FOR ME!!
<ISUZU-SAN! OUR BULLETS ARE HAVING NO EFFECT!>
BLAM!
BLAM!
I'LL FILE A REPORT ABOUT IT--LATER!
SCHRECK!
MUST BE OPEN-SEASON ON ME DOWN IN CYBORG-VILLE!
ALL I HAD TO DO WAS MESS UP WITH THEIR CUS-TOMS OFFICERS IN YOUR NAME, WOLVERINE--
IF OL' PIERCE HADN'T GOT TERMINATED BY A SENTINEL...*
...I'D SAY HE WAS STILL PROCESSIN' 'EM THROUGH HIS ELECTROLYTE VATS!
WHAT'RE YOU, AN OFF-BRAND?
* IN UNCANNY X-MEN #281--B.H.
I'M CYLLA!
AND I'M PIERCE'S LAST LITTLE PROJECT!
SPANG!
I WAS LESS THAN A VEGETABLE WITH PAIN-RECEPTORS, AND PIERCE PUT ME BACK TOGETHER--
--AND IN RETURN, I GOTTA TAKE YOU APART!

YOU'RE AT A DISADVANTAGE, SUNFIRE...!
HOW SO, GAMBIT?
YOU CAN'T UNLEASH YOUR FULL POWER INSIDE DIS BUILDING, OR YOU BRING DE WHOLE T'ING DOWN ON US, LIKE SAMSON!
I DON'T REQUIRE THE USE OF MY AWESOME SUN POWER TO DEAL WITH LOW-BORN RIFF-RAFF SUCH AS THESE NINJA!

...ALL THEM OTHER CYBORGS--ALL THEM REAVERS AND EVEN YOUR PAL DEATH-STRIKE--
--THEY WERE JUST PROTO-TYPES!
CHAK! CHAK! CHUK! SCHAUK!
I'M THE PRODUCTION MODEL!
MY CLAWS ARE LAMINATED MOLYBIDIUM STEEL!
I HAVE AN INBOARD COM-PUTER FOR SLASH TRAJECTORY!
MY EYES HAVE BUILT IN HUDS*, PRO-JECTING RANGING DATA AND TARGET PARALLAX ON MY CORNEAS!
GZASH!
* HEADS UP DISPLAY
I DON'T NEED TO OWE PIERCE TO TAKE YOU OUT, WOLVERINE--
--I'D DO IT JUST TO KNOW I'M ALIVE!

<--BACK-UP FORCE SECURING MAIN ENTRANCE AND SECONDARY EGRESS POINTS!>
POP
SQUAK
<NINJA REIN-FORCEMENTS ACCESSING ROPONGI POLICE STATION FROM THE ROOF AS ORDERED!>
<DISPENSE WITH THE PROGRESS REPORTS.>
<NOTIFY ME WHEN YOU HAVE WOLVERINE'S HEAD NEATLY WRAPPED IN A PICNIC NAPKIN.>
THESE NINJAS MAY BE LOW-BORN, AN' THEY MAY BE RIFF-RAFF--
--BUT THEY SURE BE A LOT OF THEM, HEIN?

THE DRIVER AND GUARD ARE BOUGHT BY THE HAND. THEY THINK THEY ARE FLEEING A MURDER SCENE.
THEY ARE WRONG.
I GIVE YOU BACK YOUR LIFE, MISS JUBILATION LEE --
--THIS MEANS THAT YOU ARE NOW UNDER OBLIGATION TO THE MAN YOU CALL WOLVY, THE MAN I KNEW AS PATCH!
SAY WHAT?
TELL HIM THAT REIKO PAYS HIM BACK FOR HIS MERCY AT THE GRAVEYARD IN OSAKA!*
* WOLVERINE #33!
...THIS MAKES TWICE THAT I HAVE BETRAYED THE HAND.
I AM TRULY A LOSING HAND! HA HA HA HA HA!
THAT'S RIGHT! GO OFF AND LEAVE ME HANGING!
WHAT'S SO DARN FUNNY --?
SHE IS YAKUZA --A GAMBLER. YA-KU-ZA ARE THE NUMBERS 8-9-3...
WHO...?
...AND THAT CONSTITUTES A LOSING HAND IN A COMMON CARD GAME.
IT IS, LIKE YOU SAY... "BORN TO LOSE"?
HELLO. I AM CALLED YUKIO, AND ANY FRIEND OF WOLVERINE IS A FRIEND OF MINE!
HOW COME HE DOESN'T KNOW ANY PLAIN GIRLS WITH FRUMPY TASTES IN CLOTHES --?
--DON'T ANSWER THAT!
NEXT: RAMPAGE!

MARVEL COMICS
WOLVERINE
ON SALE TWICE A MONTH!
$1.75 US
$2.15 CAN
56
EARLY JULY
UK £1.20
APPROVED BY THE COMICS CODE AUTHORITY
30TH ANNIVERSARY
1962 1992
THE AMAZING SPIDER-MAN
SILVESTRI
DG

PIECE O' CAKE.
HOP OVER TO TOKYO, BAIL JUBILEE OUT O' JAIL AND SHIP MY BIKE HOME...
...NO PROB, RIGHT?
RRRRIPP!
WRONG.
I GOTTA GET AMBUSHED BY A CYBORG...
...WHO SENT HERSELF TO ME AIR-FREIGHT AND STIFFED ME FOR THE IMPORT DUTY!
ADS .02 -
0101
2.2
006 LOCK
BACK OFF, CYLLA!
I AIN'T PARTIAL TO SLICIN' ON LADIES!
OH MY! AREN'T WE THE GENTLEMAN!
MAYBE THERE ISN'T ENOUGH ORIGINAL ORGANIC TISSUE LEFT IN ME TO QUALIFY FOR THAT DISTINCTION!
SKRANG!
'SAID I WASN'T PARTIAL--
--DIDN'T SAY I WASN'T WILLIN'!
An adventure of the Canadian X-MAN by-
LARRY HAMA WRITER
MARC SILVESTRI PENCILER
DAN GREEN INKER
PAT BROSSEAU LETTERER
STEVE BUCCELLATO COLORIST
BOB HARRAS EDITOR
TOM DEFALCO EDITOR IN CHIEF

WE GOTCYLLA,
CAN MOTHRA BE FAR BEHIND ?
SO MUCH FOR THE PLEASANT CHIT CHAT--
--LET'S GET DOWN TO SOME SERIOUS SLASH AND BASH, HERE!
SCHRACKK!
YOU DON'T GET IT, DO YOU?
FLESH AND BLOOD DON'T NEED A REASON TO BE ALIVE--
--MACHINES ARE PUT TOGETHER FOR A PURPOSE!
AIN'T NO RAPTURE MORE ECSTATIC THAN A MACHINE/INTELLIGENCE INTERFACE FULFILLING ITS INTENDED PURPOSE!
SO YOU GET YOUR JOLLIES BY KILLIN'?
BRRAPP
YOU GOTTA BE A SICK PUPPY, LADY--

UNGH!
WHAT'S YOUR PROBLEM, LADY?
I DON'T EVEN KNOW YOU!
YOU REALLY THINK YOU OWE PIERCE FOR HOT-RODDIN' YOU UP INTO A SUPER-TOASTER?
BRARRRRRRR!
SPANG!
--HERE! TAKE THIS UNDER THE PORCH AND PLAY WITH IT!
IF THIS WERE A CHEAP MELODRAMA, I'D BE TELLING YOU RIGHT NOW THAT I WAS "THROUGH PLAYING WITH YOU"--
--BUT THE TRUTH IS, THAT THE FUN'S JUST BEGUN!

AND, UP ON THE ROOF...
<STOP! IT IS OUR SWORN DUTY AS POLICEMEN TO PROTECT HELP-LESS CITIZENS!>
<SUNFIRE HAS THE POWER TO PROJECT SOLAR FIRE. HE IS HARDLY HELPLESS!>
<AND THAT TALL GAIJIN IS NO CITIZEN!>
<IF MUTANTS, FOREIGNERS AND NINJA ASSASSINS FROM THE HAND INSIST ON KILLING EACH OTHER IN OUR POLICE STATION-- MORE POWER TO THEM!>
INSIDE, THE POLICE STATION.
EEEYAH! I AM INSULTED, GAMBIT-SAN!
WE ARE NOT THE OBJECTIVES OF THESE HAND NINJAS--!
--THEY MEAN TO GET PAST US, TO SLAY WOLVERINE!
C'EST VRAI, SUNFIRE, MON AMI!
THEY SPIT ON YOUR HONNEUR! PAY THEM BACK WITH SOME OF THAT POWER I HEAR ABOUT!
YOU KNOW I DARE NOT!
MY PLASMA CONVERSION BEAM WOULD PIERCE THE WALLS AND ENDANGER INNOCENT CIVILIANS!

DOMMAGE COLLATERAL?
IT IS A MATTER OF DIRECTION, NON?
'SCUSE ME, WHILE I CHARGE UP A HIGH STRAIGHT--
--AND CLEAR A PATCH O' FLOOR SPACE FOR YOU!
BLAST US A TRENCH, HOMME--
AHH! WAKARIMASHITA!* A TRENCH DEEP ENOUGH TO FLING NINJAS INTO!
* I UNDERSTAND!

WHAT'S TAKING SO LONG IN THERE? YOU ONLY NEED TO CHOP OFF *ONE* HEAD...
...DIDN'T I BUY OFF ENOUGH POLICEMEN?
UNEXPECTED INTERFERENCE, TSURAYABA-SAMA!
SHOW ME!
MONITOR FEED #3! THE TALL GAIJIN AND THE *MUTANT RONIN!*
I KNEW THAT THE X-MAN, *GAMBIT* WAS HERE, BUT WHAT BUSINESS IS THIS OF *SUNFIRE'S?*
THESE *MUTANTS* ARE SO *CLANNISH!*

INSIDE.
COME ON, MUTANT!
ADAMANTIUM MAY BE THE HARDEST STUFF AROUND, BUT WHAT ABOUT THE LITTLE GUY THAT'S WRAPPED AROUND IT?
I AIN'T WRAPPED...

...I'M BONDED!
THWAM!

YESSSS!!!
I KNEW YOU HAD THE KILLER RAGE IN-SIDE!
EEEYAA!
LET IT OUT! LET IT OUT!

LET'S ROCK AND ROLL!
SPANG!
SCHRAKK!

PANK
<I JUST FOUND OUT WHERE WOLVERINE IS! HE'S IN ONE OF THE BACK ROOMS!>
<GET BACK THERE-->
SPOK

<--AND HARVEST HIS HEAD!>
<IT SHALL BE DONE, LORD!>

<BROTHERS OF THE HAND! OUR JONIN WAXES IMPATIENT FOR HIS PRIZE!>
<MATSUO WANTS TO MAKE A TEACUP FROM THE GAIJIN'S SKULL!>
<THEN HE SHALL HAVE IT!>
<IF YOU ASK ME, A TEACUP FOR A RIGHT HAND IS A BAD TRADE!>
<IF MATSUO HEARD THAT, HE'D HAVE YOUR LIVER!>

<YOU WOULDN'T REPORT ME, WOULD YOU--?>
<NO.>
<JUST FOLLOW ME.>

<WE'RE GOING TO GET ABOVE THEM AND DROP DOWN ON TOP OF THEM WITH THESE CLAWS?>
<DON'T BE ABSURD! WE ARE GOING TO SNEAK PAST THEM ACROSS THE CEILING AND GET OUR JONIN'S TEA-CUP!>

THIS IS WHAT MY EXIS-TENCE IS ALL ABOUT!
THWAMM!
EVERY OUNCE OF ME THAT AIN'T DEVOTED TO FIGHTING IS JUST THERE TO GET ME TO THE FIGHT!
I KNOW WHAT YOU NEED, LADY--
--SHUT UP!
THWOMP!
JUST PLAIN OLD KILLING DON'T DO IT FOR ME!
I NEED THE CHALLENGE OF AN OPPONENT WITH CHOPS AND HEART!
I NEED A RUN FOR MY MONEY!
I NEED COMBAT WITH AN EDGE!
SHUT UP, AND GET UP!
YOU STILL GOT A MESS O' FIGHT LEFT IN YOU...
...AND I AIM TO GET IT ALL!

THESE NINJAS ARE CREEPING PAST US 'CROSS THE CEILING, HOMME!

WORSE THAN CAFARDS, NON?
WHAT WE CALL GOKIBURI-- COCK-ROACHES!
ANNOYING, DISGUSTING CREATURES...
...BUT EASILY SWATTED!

RRRRUMBLE
<EARTHQUAKE?>
<NO, JONIN! IT IS THE ADVENTURER, SUNFIRE -->

<--SEE HIS ENERGY BEAM PIERCE THE SKY!>
SUNFIRE, MON AMI-- DO YOU KNOW WHAT AN INTERIOR LOAD-BEARING CANTILEVER BEAM IS?
YES. IT IS USED TO CREATE OPEN SPACES WITH-OUT PILLARS LIKE THIS CEN-TRAL BOOKING ROOM. WHY?
YOU JUST BURNED RIGHT THROUGH IT, HOMME--!

...I WOULD HAVE HAD THE PLACE BLOWN UP IN THE FIRST PLACE!

GET ME OUT OF HERE!

WE'RE NOT GONNA LET A LITTLE OL' EARTH-QUAKE SHUT DOWN OUR LITTLE RUMPUS, ARE WE?

POP THEM CLAWS! LET'S GET DOWN TO--

--BUSINESS, MA PETITE?

P'RAPS YOU'D LIKE TO DEAL US IN FOR THIS HAND--OR IS THIS A CLOSED GAME?
YOU SEEM HARD-PRESSED, WOLVERINE!
WOULD YOU LIKE ME TO MELT AWAY SOME OF HER WEAPONRY?
URRRRG!
I'LL BE BACK!
THERE'S NO-WHERE FOR ONE LIKE HER TO HIDE IN TOKYO--
WE CAN CHASE HER DOWN AND--
FORGET HER!
WE CAME TO FIND JUBILEE...
...DID SHE DISAPPEAR INTO THE WOODWORK, OR WHAT?

IN ANOTHER PART OF TOKYO...
'THIS YOUR HOUSE, YUKIO?
I HAVE A ROOM HERE.
WE CAN HIDE YOU HERE UNTIL WE FIGURE OUT EXACTLY WHAT'S GOING ON--

...I HEARD THAT THE HAND WAS LOOKING FOR A FREE-LANCER TO PULL A HIT ON AN AMERICAN JUVENILE-- THOUGHT I SHOULD LOOK INTO IT...
...AN ADVENTURER HAS TO KEEP HER EYES OPEN, JUBILATION-SAN!
EVERYONE CALLS ME JUBILEE...

...GOSH. KINDA COZY, HUH?
I HATE DISSEMBLERS.
THIS PLACE IS A DUMP AND YOU KNOW IT.
ADVENTURING DOESN'T PAY MUCH IN JAPAN.

WHAT'S YOUR PROBLEM? GOT A CRUSH ON LOGAN?

WHAT'S YOUR PROBLEM?
I BET YOU AND HIM USED TO HAVE A THING! BUT HE'S NOT WITH YOU NOW--!
--IS HE?

LET'S TALK ABOUT SOMETHING ELSE--

OKAY--YOU ALWAYS HAVE THIS MANY COP-CARS SPEEDING THROUGH YOUR 'HOOD?
THEY'RE HEADING FOR ROPONGI. SOMETHING BIG MUST BE HAPPENING THERE...
ROPONGI POLICE STATION WAS WHERE WOLVIE WAS SUPPOSED TO PICK ME UP!

WE HAD BETTER GET DOWN THERE!
NEED ANYTHING?

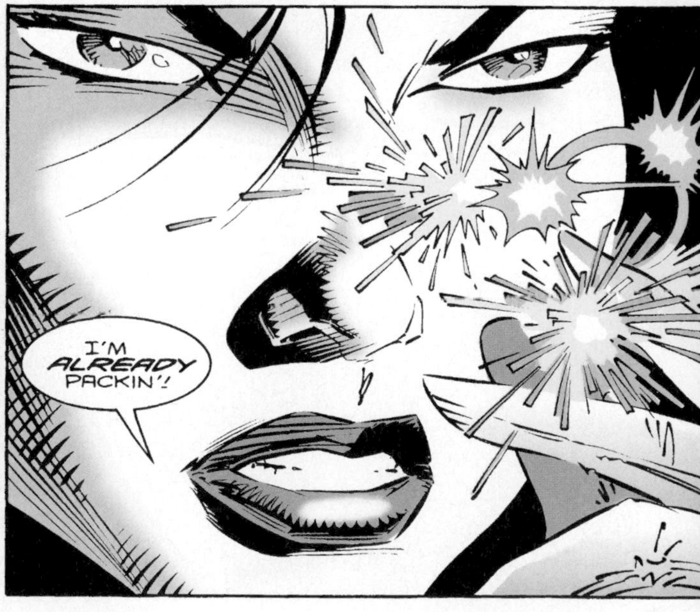
I'M ALREADY PACKIN'!

AT THE TOKYO DOCKS...
<I CHECKED YOU OUT THROUGH MY SOURCES, KOJIRO. I KNOW YOU'RE NOT CONNECTED TO THE HAND. YOU'RE A FREELANCER, LIKE ME...>
<...CAN YOU FIX IT SO I CAN STOW AWAY ON THIS SHIP? I NEED TO SLIP OUT OF JAPAN, UNNOTICED-->
<DEPENDS.>
<HOW ANGRY DID YOU MAKE THE HAND?>
<I WAS SUPPOSED TO KILL AN AMERICAN-BORN CHINESE GIRL FOR THEM. IT TURNS OUT SHE IS A FRIEND OF SOMEONE I AM INDEBTED TO. I HAD TO RENEGE ON THE CONTRACT-->
<OFFERED YOU YOUR EYES BACK, DID HE? MATSUO, THAT IS...>
<YES-- HOW DID-->
<I HAVE MY SOURCES, TOO.>
<YOU'RE NOT LONG FOR THIS WORLD, GIRL. I WANT MY MONEY UP FRONT!>
<THIS IS ALL I HAVE. MY MOTHER'S PEARLS, SOME JADE-->
<WORTHLESS TRINKETS! GOT ANY YEN? SWISS FRANCS? KRUGER-RANDS?>
<NOTHING! I HAVE NOTHING-->
<TOO BAD! IF YOU HAD ENOUGH CASH, I'D HAVE LET YOU SLIDE, BUT TIMES ARE TOUGH, KID--AND BUSINESS IS BUSINESS!>
<SHE'S ALL YOURS, BOYS-->
<I THOUGHT YOU WEREN'T CONNECTED TO THE HAND!>

<I'M NOT...>
<...BUT HYDRA-- THAT'S ANOTHER STORY!>
JUST COME ALONG QUIETLY, GIRLIE! WE DON'T WANT TO HURT YOU!
YOU'RE GOING TO CHANGE YOUR MINDS ABOUT THAT--
--REAL SOON!
ZISH!
ZASH!
ARRRRRGH!
I WANT HER ALIVE! BE CAREFUL! HER SWORD IS COATED WITH BLOWFISH TOXIN!
QUICK! THE ANTIDOTE!
THERE IS NONE. IF THE DOSAGE ISN'T SUFFICIENT FOR INSTANTANEOUS BRAIN DEATH, EXPIRATION CAN BE PROLONGED AND EXCRUCIATING--
AIIIIEEEE!
I'LL TAKE CARE OF THIS...
...BUT IT'S GONNA COST YOU EXTRA!

I JUST CONTRACTED FOR DELIVERY--
--NOT FOR GIFT-WRAPPING!
YOU ALSO MIGHT HAVE WARNED ME ABOUT THE BLOWFISH TOXIN!
CONSIDER IT A TEST THAT YOU HAVE PASSED.
LOOK AT ME, GIRL. YOU ARE ONE REIKO, LATE OF THE DAI-KUMO CLAN IN OSAKA?
WHO WANTS TO KNOW?
ZORA DE PLATA...
...SILVER FOX TO YOU. I HAVE NEED OF A POISONER OF YOUR SKILL. AND HYDRA WILL BE EVER SO GRATEFUL--
--AND WHO ELSE BUT HYDRA COULD HELP YOU EVADE THE HAND, HMMMM?

ROPONGI...
...I GUESS WHEN THEY HAVE A JAIL-BREAK OVER HERE, THEY REALLY MEAN IT!
WOLVERINE DIDN'T DO THIS. THERE WERE OTHERS HERE WITH EXTENSIVE POWERS...
WHOSE SIDE WERE THEY ON? AND WHERE DID WOLVIE GO OFF TO?
SHHHH! BACK INTO THE SHADOWS! I RECOGNIZE THAT LIMO!
THE TWO GAIJIN DEPARTED WITH SUNFIRE, O LORD! THEY WERE NOT IN ACCORD!
WITHOUT THE AID OF SUNFIRE OR THE GOVERNMENT, THEY WILL BE FORCED TO GO TO OTHERS FOR AID IN FINDING THE BRAT-- YOU DID DISPOSE OF THE BRAT?
THERE WERE COMPLICATIONS, JONIN--
I THINK WE HAD BEST KEEP TABS ON MATSUO!

STOP!
YOU CAN'T JUST COME BARGING INTO THIS COUNTRY, DESTROY GOVERNMENT PROPERTY AND BLITHELY RIDE OFF INTO THE NIGHT!
JUST WATCH ME, BUB!
WE DIDN'T START IT, SUNFIRE!
SOMEBODY HAS TO TAKE THE RESPONSIBILI-TY!
YOU'RE THE ONE WHO UNLEASHED MEGA-BOLTS AND TRASHED THE PLACE!
WHO ASKED FOR YOUR HELP IN THE FIRST PLACE?
SKREEEEE!
WE'LL SETTLE THIS LATER!
WHERE TO NOW, EH?
WE GO TALK TO SOMEBODY WHO HAS JUICE IN THIS TOWN!

<...SO, YOU ALL THINK THE YASHIDA CLAN HAS SO MUCH "POWER"-->
<--THAT THE HAND CAN'T PUSH US AROUND?>
<WHAT IS MERE POLITICAL INFLUENCE AGAINST SHEER RUTHLESSNESS AND IMMENSE WEALTH?>
<THE POLITICIANS WHO OWE US FAVORS HAVE TOO MUCH HONOR TO BETRAY US!>
<POLITICS AND HONOR ARE MUTUALLY EXCLUSIVE TERMS, MY FRIEND.>
<WE CAN'T JUST IGNORE THE HAND! WE HAVE TO COME TO TERMS WITH THEM OR THEY WILL SWALLOW US WHOLE!>
<ARE YOU SUGGESTING MAKING A DEAL WITH THE HAND?>
<NO--!>
<I'M NOT BUCKLING UNDER THE HAND! I AM SIMPLY TRYING TO FULFILL MY PROMISE TO DIVEST THE CLAN OF UNDERWORLD HOLDINGS-->
<A PROMISE TO WHOM?>
THAT'S A PERSONAL QUESTION, BUB--
<SILVER SAMURAI! HOW DID YOU GET INSIDE--?>
<SHINGEN WAS MY FATHER, TOO! THOUGH HE DENIED ME MY BIRTHRIGHT, HE DID BEQUEATH ME A FEW SECRETS!>
<MARIKO LIES! THAT IS EXACTLY WHAT THIS FALSE OYABUN SUGGESTS!>
<I HAVE COME TO SAVE THE YASHIDAS FROM THE HAND! NAME ME CLAN LEADER AND IT SHALL BE RUN AS IT SHOULD BE RUN--BY A MAN!>

LOGAN-SAN!
--MARIKO, IS THIS CREEP GIVIN' YOU A HASSLE?
IF HE IS, I'M GONNA HAVE TO TAKE HIS SWORD AWAY FROM HIM AND SPANK HIM WITH IT!
YOU DARE TO DEFAME MY INVINCIBLE BLACK BLADE?
THAT SNICKERSNEE CAN CUT THROUGH EVERYTHING EXCEPT ADAMANTIUM, BUB--AND DON'T YOU FORGET IT!
STOP! I WILL NOT ALLOW THE TWO OF YOU TO SHED EACH OTHERS' BLOOD IN MY HOUSE!
ALARM! NINJAS! THE HAND HAS US SUR-ROUNDED!

AND, OUTSIDE:

< WE ARE SENDING IN AN ENVOY WITH YOUR ULTIMATUM, LORD! IS THERE ANY PERSONAL MESSAGE YOU WOULD INCLUDE? >

< TELL MARIKO THAT I KNOW HER WILL HAS BEEN SAPPED BY HER STUPID PROMISE TO THE GAIJIN! >

< SHE MIGHT AS WELL COME CRAWLING OUT WITH THE NAPE OF HER NECK EXTENDED FOR THE BEHEADING CUT! >

MARVEL COMICS
ON SALE TWICE A MONTH!
$1.75 US
$2.15 CAN
57
LATE JULY
02254
APPROVED BY THE COMICS CODE AUTHORITY
SALVESTRI DG

TOKYO.
YASHIDA MANSION COMPOUND.
WHY IS MATSUO SENDING HIS HAND NINJAS TO ASSAULT MARIKO'S HOME? THEY WERE IN THE MIDST OF NEGOTIATIONS!
YOU MIGHT SAY THAT I HAD A HAND IN THIS, SILVER SAMURAI!
AN ITCH THAT DON'T GO AWAY, GAMBIT!
THAT IS TO SAY, THAT MATSUO HAS AN ITCH WHERE HIS FINGERS USED TO BE, N'EST-CE-PAS?
MATSUO MAY HAVE A PERSONAL SCORE TO SETTLE WITH LOGAN...
DEATH IN THE FAMILY!
LARRY HAMA SCRIPT • MARC SILVESTRI PENCILER • GREEN/MILGROM RUBINSTEIN INKERS • PAT BROSSEAU LETTERER • STEVE BUCCELLATO COLORIST • BOB HARRAS EDITOR • TOM DEFALCO ED. IN. CHIEF

... BUT HE ALSO WANTS THE YASHIDA CLAN UNDERWORLD CONNECTIONS INTACT FOR THE HAND!
AND THAT'S SOMETHIN' YOU DON'T WANT TO HAND OVER, IS IT, MARIKO, DARLIN'?
NOT WHILE I CAN STILL HOLD THE HONOR SWORD OF THE YASHIDA CLAN!
TOO MANY!
WE MUST FORCE OUR WAY OUT! MAINTENANT!
NO! FALL BACK, INSIDE THE MANSION!
NO ROOM TO MANEUVER! WE'LL BE TRAPPED!
A YASHIDA CAN'T BE TRAPPED IN A HOUSE BUILT BY SHINGEN!
POURQOI?
WHY? 'CAUSE SHINGEN WAS A MASTER OF MANY A FIENDISH WEAPON...
... BUT HIS HOUSE WAS THE DEADLIEST!
AIEEEE!
THWUMP!
CHAK!

THIS IS TAKING TOO LONG! I CAN'T KEEP THE AUTHORITIES AT BAY MUCH LONGER...
...AND WHO KNOWS HOW LONG IT WILL TAKE TO WINKLE THE LOT OF THEM OUT OF THAT WEASEL WARREN!
LONGER THAN YOU'VE GOT, MATSUO TSURAYABA!
...UNLESS YOU CHANGE YOUR TACTICS AND USE CUNNING INSTEAD OF BRUTE FORCE!
SOMEONE APPROACHES MY LIMOUSINE!
WHO--?
JUST ANOTHER ARM OF THE MANY-TENTACLED HYDRA!
I BELIEVE THIS SIGHTLESS WAIF IS ONE OF YOURS?
AND, HIDDEN IN THE BUSHES.
OOOOH, YUKIO! THAT BLIND GIRL IS REIKO! MATSUO SICCED HER ON ME AND SHE LET ME GO 'CAUSE SHE KNEW WOLVY--
--THEN SHE WOULD WANT YOU TO KEEP GOING AND TRY TO GET TO HIM, JUBILEE!!
COME! WE TAKE TO THE ROOFTOPS!

THE COMPOUND...

RAZOR BLADES IMBEDDED IN THE WALLS...?

...OF A MAZE?

I AM NOT SO IMPRESSED, WOLVERINE. ONE JUS' HAS TO BE CARE-FUL--

YEAH, WELL, THAT BEIN' CARE-FUL PART AIN'T SO EASY AFTER THEY TURN OUT THE LIGHTS AND LET LOOSE THE STARVIN' DOGS!

THIS IS THE CORE OF THE MANSION, SHINSEN'S IMPREGNABLE CITADEL.

EXCUSE US, PLEASE. LOGAN AND I HAVE IMPORTANT MATTERS TO DISCUSS IN THE PRIVACY OF THE CHAPEL.

I DON'T LIKE THIS!

THAT'S WHY THEY DOIN' IT, HOMME!

...HAVE YOU RETURNED TO SHAME ME?
AFTER ALL THIS TIME, I HAVE NOT YET SUCCEEDED IN DIVESTING THE YASHIDA CLAN OF ITS UNDER-WORLD HOLDINGS.
I AM DISHONOR-ED--
NO DISHONOR, DARLIN'--
--THINGS HAPPEN, IS ALL.
I AM VERY CLOSE TO ACCOMPLISHING MY TASK: TO CLEANSE MY CLAN SO THAT I MAY BE WORTHY--
IT IS SO COMPLICATED. SO MANY FAMLIES WITHIN THE CLAN AND I AM RESPONSIBLE FOR THEIR WELL-BEING...
IS
PACKIN',
--
I HAVEN'T SEEN THAT SET O' COLORS IN A WHILE. GAVE 'EM UP, MARIKO.
PERHAPS IT IS FITTING FOR YOU TO WEAR THEM AGAIN TO SERVE THE HONOR OF THE YASHIDA CLAN?

OUTSIDE...
BRING ME THAT TRAITOROUS POISONER SO THAT I MAY THROTTLE HER PERSONALLY--
WHAT!?
CHUNG
NOT SO FAST! YOU DON'T GET TO CHOKE THE MERCHANDISE UNTIL YOU PAY FOR IT--
I ALREADY OWN HER, YOU CRETIN!
FOOM!
TRUE, THE GIRL IS YOURS TO KILL, BUT SHE IS ALSO THE MEANS TO YOUR ENDS! CAN WE TALK?
I DON'T DEAL WITH NAMELESS ENTITIES.
CALL ME SILVER FOX.
NNNGGGHH!

THAT'S WHERE WOLVERINE PROBABLY IS.
DEEP WITHIN THE TRAP-RIDDLED LABYRINTH KNOWN AS SHINGEN'S CITADEL. JUST ACROSS THE STREET...
GREAT. WHAT ARE WE GONNA DO, YUKIO, FLY?
NO. POWER LINE.
ULP! ARE YOU SURE THIS IS SAFE??
JUST DON'T GROUND YOURSELF!
WHY WOULD I DO THAT? I LIKE GOING OUT--
QUIET! THAT'S MATSUO'S LIMO BELOW US!
AND ME WITHOUT A BRICK--
WHAT NOW? ISN'T THIS THE RIGHT ROOF?
YES ...
BUT THERE'S SOME-BODY OR SOMETHING UP HERE WITH US!

INSIDE...
MEN OF THE YASHIDA CLAN! HAVE YOU NO SHAME, THAT YOU ALLOW YOURSELVES TO BE LED BY A WOMAN?
HAS SHE EVER PROVEN HER HONOR? HAS SHE CUT OFF A FINGER IN ATONEMENT FOR HER COMPLICITY IN THE DEATH OF SHINGEN?
SHE WAS EVEN BETROTHED TO SHINGEN'S KILLER--
I'VE AGREED TO THIS EMBARRASSMENT LONG ENOUGH--
LAY OFF, HOMME!
THE MAN ISN'T EVEN HERE TO DEFEND HIMSELF FROM YOUR SLURS--
I AM, NOW!
THE SILENT ALARMS HAVE BEEN TRIGGERED! THE HAND HAVE ENTERED THE MANSION!
THE SENSORS INDICATE THAT IT IS BUT A SINGLE INTRUDER...

"...SOMEONE SMALL-- LIKE A GIRL!"
--I UNDERSTAND REIKO BLOODING HER SWORD FOR US TO BUY HER EYES BACK...
...BUT ISN'T SHE UNDER OBLIGATION TO WOLVERINE?
SHE DOESN'T KNOW ABOUT HIS RELATIONSHIP TO MARIKO.
TAP
TAP
YOU HAVE LET YOUR HATRED RUN AMOK...
"...LIKE A PACK OF STARVING DOGS."
GRRRRRR!
SOMETHING ELSE OUT THERE...SOMETHING STRONG, BUT ALIEN--
ZISH!

"--UP ON THE ROOF!"
I SAW SOMETHING MOVING UP THERE, YUKIO!
TOO DARK AND THE RAIN IS TOO HEAVY! CAN'T SEE--
NO PROB!
PAF! PAF!
I'LL JUST POP SOME LIGHT ON THE SITUATION AND--
IT TOOK OFF ON WARP NINE!
WHATEVER IT IS, I SURE HOPE IT'S NOT STALKING WOLVY! HE'S GOT ENOUGH TO WORRY ABOUT RIGHT NOW--
IT'S BEHIND US, JUBILEE!
WHO OR WHAT IS THAT?
I'LL TELL YOU WHAT I AM...

...I'M THE LAST THING YOU'LL SEE IN THIS LIFE!
ESPECIALLY SINCE YOU'RE PALS O' WOLVERINE!
EEP!
THOOM!!
THANKS, YUKIO!
GET YOURSELF TOGETHER! WE'RE NOT OUT OF THIS YET!
WOLVERINE! LOOK WHO I'VE GOT UP HERE! COME ON UP AN' WATCH WHILE I MINCE THEM!
THAT MANIAC CYBORG CYLLA HAS JUBE AND YUKIO!
BEST GET UP THERE, MON AMI!
WE DON'T KNOW WHAT'S COMIN' THROUGH THE MAZE! I CAN'T LEAVE MARIKO--
I LOOK AFTER HER! GO SAVE THOSE GIRLS ON THE ROOF!
I GIVE YOU A BOOST!
A BOOST? FIFTY FEET WORTH?

ANYBODY ELSE, HE GIVE YOU A BOOST...
SNIKT!
...HE AIN'T GOT THE POWER!
SENDIN' ME UP LIKE A BIG GAME O' 52-PICKUP...?
SNIKT!
...THAT'S JAKE WITH THE OL' CANUCKLE-HEAD, LONG AS HE'S GOT ALL THE ACES!
HEADS UP, CYLLA!
YOU WANTED A FIGHT, NOW YOU GOT IT--
--IN SPADES!

AND, BELOW...
THIS IS THE INTRUDER WHO SAFELY TRAVERSED SHINGEN'S MAZE?
C'EST UNE JEUNE FILLE DANGEREUX...
SALUTATIONS FROM TSURAYABA MATSUO OF THE HAND!
I AM REIKO, A FREE AGENT, FORMERLY OF THE DAI-KUMO GROUP IN OSAKA. I AM EMPOWERED TO MAKE A PROPOSITION...
...MATSUO OFFERS TO BUY OUT YASHIDA CLAN UNDERWORLD HOLDINGS AT FAIR-MARKET VALUE AND HE WILL DISSOLVE THOSE HOLDINGS SO THAT MARIKO WILL NOT BE PROFITING FROM VICE--
--EXCUSE ME. WHAT IS THAT COMMOTION ABOVE US?

THAT IS NONE OF YOUR CONCERN!
THIS IS A GENEROUS OFFER. IT ALLOWS ME TO FULFILL MY VOW TO DIVEST WITHOUT FINANCIALLY RUINING THE FAMLIES OF MY CLAN...!
...WHAT DOES MATSUO WANT IN RETURN?

HE WANTS YOU TO MAKE ATONEMENT IN THE MANNER OF THE YAKUZA...

...HE WANTS ONE OF YOUR FINGERS.

TOO BAD YOU'RE SO PROMPT, SPORT--
--I WAS FIXING TO ENJOY SLICING AND DICING YOUR LITTLE PALS!
ZASH!
YOU LIKE BEIN' A SICK PUPPY, DON'T YOU?
SSCHREK!
"...PIERCE GAVE ME STATE-OF-THE-ART CYBORG WEAPONS SYSTEMS!
"I CAN TRACK YOU IN THE DARK FROM YOUR INFRARED SIGNATURE AND MY TARGETING SUITE IS--"
--I HEARD THIS RAP THE LAST TIME!
'TRUTH IS, IF YOU WAS TRULY THE MASTER OF ALL THAT FANCY HARDWARE...
...YOU WOULDN'T BE NEEDIN' TO USE IT ALL THE TIME!
IT AIN'T SICK TO DO WHAT YOU'RE MADE FOR...!
ARRRRRRRGH!
SKRRRAK!

THIS IS BARBARIC! COME BACK DOWN HERE AND STOP THEM, MON AMI!
WHO ARE YOU SPEAKING TO UP THERE?
YOU WERE TOLD THAT IS NONE OF YOUR CONCERN!
SPAK!
THOK!
IS THIS THE BLADE THAT MATSUO OFFERS FOR THE FINGER-CUTTING?
IT IS A MURAMASA TANTO. A WORTHY BLADE--
HOW DO WE KNOW IT ISN'T POISONED? DOES MATSUO TAKE US FOR FOOLS?
THAT IS BESIDES THE POINT!
WOULD I DO THIS WITH SULLIED STEEL?
THUNK!
NOW, MARIKO OYABUN--
--IT IS YOUR TURN!

IF I WERE INCLINED TO USE CHESS METAPHORS, I'D SAY YOU WERE IN CHECK!
YOUR BACK'S TO THE RAIN-GUTTER AND YOU'VE GOT NO ROOM TO MANEUVER--
GIRL, YOU GOT A FACE FULL O' UGLY AND A MOUTH FULL O' "I'M GONNA GETCHA"!
HOWSABOUT GETTIN' DOWN WITH THE OL' CLAWS? LET'S GO FOR IT, CYLLA! TURN ON THAT ELECTRONIC TARGETING SYSTEM YOU'VE BEEN BRAGGIN' ON--!
"YOU'RE ALREADY SIGHTED IN, WOLVERINE--"
PAF
PAF
PAF
I'LL KEEP FRYING HER VISION RECEPTORS, YOU HAUL HIM IN, YUKIO!
UNGH! I DON'T NEED TO SEE YOU TO--
--URK!
WATCH OUT FOR THAT FIRST STEP--
--IT'S A KILLER!

YA KNOW, THERE'S A LIL' DEVIL SITTIN' ON MY SHOULDER, SHOUTIN', "GO AHEAD! KICK HER IN THE FACE! WATCH HER FALL DOWN, GO BOOM!"
KRUNK!
KREEEEEEE!
TRY IT, MUTANT! I'LL BITE IT OFF!
DEEP INSIDE, YOU'RE WEAK! YOU AIN'T GOT THE GUTS TO DO ME IN COLD BLOOD! THAT'S WHY I'M GONNA WIN!
BELOW...
YOU ARE CORRECT, REIKO ...
THOK!
... IT IS TIME FOR MARIKO YASHIDA TO MAKE THINGS RIGHT FOR ALL THOSE WHO HAVE PUT THEIR TRUST IN HER!
THE LIMO...
I SEE THAT WOLVERINE HAS BEEN DISTRACTED FROM THE MAIN EVENT WITH THE POISONED BLADE--
YES. I ARRANGED FOR THAT.

ALOR! YOU CAN'T LET HER--
SHE MUST DO THIS!
AM I MISSING SOME-THING?
WON'T THEY DEMAND THAT THE BLADE BE TESTED ON REIKO, FIRST?
REIKO HAS BEEN GRADUALLY INGESTING MINUTELY LARGER DOSES OF THE TOXIN FOR YEARS...
"...SHE IS QUITE IMMUNE!"
AIEEEEEEEEEEEEEEEE!
IT BURNS--! LIKE WHITE FIRE RUN-NING UP MY VEINS!
BLOWFISH TOXIN! BUT HOW--?
THAT'S MARIKO!!
GO TO HER LOGAN!
JUBILEE AND I WILL DEAL WITH THE CYBORG!

MARIKO!
LOGAN, MY BELOVED! TAKE ME INTO THE CHAPEL!

LOGAN! LOGAN IS MARIKO'S BELOVED--
--WHAT HAVE I DONE?

HOW WERE YOU PLANNING TO EXTRACT REIKO FROM THIS SCENARIO?
THAT PROBLEM IS SOLVING ITSELF ...

"...RIGHT ABOUT NOW!"
IS THERE NO PEACE--

--OTHER THAN THE LONG DARKNESS?
SHUK!

I AM POISONED, MY BELOVED--
LET'S GET YOU TO A HOSPITAL, DARLIN'--!
GET THE ANTIDOTE--!
THERE IS NONE! JUST T-TAKE ME INTO THE CHAPEL...

...IT IS A HORRIBLE ENOUGH DEATH. IT SHOULD NOT BE A PUBLIC SPECTACLE. HOLD ME.
OH, LOGAN--I MUST ASK OF YOU ONE FINAL BOON. I HAVE FULFILLED MY VOW. I HAVE DIVESTED THE CLAN, EVEN IF THE HAND DELVED IN TREACHERY, I HAVE UPHELD MY END...
...I WOULD HAVE BEEN FREE TO MARRY YOU!
DARLIN'...
BUT AREN'T WE MARRIED IN OUR HEARTS? HAVE WE NOT PAID A DOWRY IN BLOOD AND PAIN AND LONELINESS?
ISN'T THE MOST SACRED VOW THE ONE WE CARRY IN THE CORE OF OUR SOULS?
WHAT ARE YOU ASKIN' ME, DARLIN'?
SPARE ME THE FINAL AGONIES! RE-LEASE MY SOUL WHILE IT STILL SINGS WITH MY LOVE FOR YOU!
USE YOUR CLAWS, MY BELOVED--
NO! I CAN'T!!!

ON THE ROOF...
I DON'T NEED MY VISION RECEPTORS TO FINISH OF THE LIKES OF YOU TWO--
--I'VE GOT MY AUDIO-DIRECTION-FINDERS, INFRARED DETECTORS AND PULSE-DOPPLER RADAR!
I'M GONNA--
WHAT ARE YOU DOING, YUKIO? THAT LITTLE THROWING DIRK ISN'T EVEN GOING TO MESS HER MOUSSE!
I'M TRYING TO CUT THE POWER LINE WE SLID ACROSS THE STREET ON--
TZZAP
--THAT STEADY STREAM OF WATER COURSING OVER CYLLA AND DOWN TO THE COURTYARD...
SHA-ZZAP
AAAAAAAAARGH!
...IS GOING TO GROUND HER OUT!!
SHOOMP

SNIKT
FIN

***ESSENTIAL WOLVERINE VOL. 3 TPB* (1998 1ST EDITION) COVER ART BY MICHAEL HIGGINS, KLAUS JANSON & HABERLIN STUDIOS**

WOLVERINE LEGENDS: MARC SILVESTRI TPB COVER ART BY MARC SILVESTRI & VICTOR GONZALEZ

It's a fact: when you exert yourself you sweat, and when you sweat you stink. This goes for super heroes as well. And just like ordinary people, super heroes, even those with a hypersensitive sense of smell like Wolverine, are usually the last ones to know that they smell bad. And though our product could help Wolverine with his body odor problem...

...We'd rather not be the ones to tell him.

MACHO
speed stick
deoderant

"FOR THE HERO IN US ALL"

MARVEL ILLUSTRATED: THE SWIMSUIT ISSUE PARODY AD BY MIKE ZECK

Our blades can't tear through an X91-N-M-E War-bot like Wolverine's, but we'd like to see him make a strawberry parfait with his.

X91-NME

LA PUREE

La Puree from Sharp ideas.

MARVEL SWIMSUIT SPECIAL #1 PARODY AD BY ART THIBERT & TOM SMITH

MARVEL ILLUSTRATED: THE SWIMSUIT ISSUE PINUP BY KEVIN NOWLAN • TEXT BY MAX FLEISHER

MARVEL SWIMSUIT SPECIAL #1 PINUP BY MIKE MIGNOLA & GREGORY WRIGHT • TEXT BY MATTHEW MORRA

SILVESTRI
+
GREEN